# Protectionism

The Ohlin Lectures

1. Jagdish Bhagwati, *Protectionism* (1988).

# Protectionism

Jagdish Bhagwati

The MIT Press
Cambridge, Massachusetts
London, England

This book was set in Bembo by Achorn Graphic Services and printed and bound by Halliday Lithograph in the United States of America.

Library of Congress Cataloging-in-Publication Data

Bhagwati, Jagdish N., 1934–
  Protectionism.

  (The Ohlin lectures; 1)
  Bibliography: p.
  Includes index.
  1. Free trade and protection—Protection. I. Title.
  II. Series.
  HF1713.B47   1988        382.7'3        88-672
  ISBN 0-262-02282-6

*for Padma and Anuradha*

# Contents

Preface                                          ix
Introduction                                     xi

1
Postwar Liberalization                            1

2
Ideology, Interests, and Institutions            17

3
The Rise of Protectionism                        43

4
Structural Change and Interdependence            61

5
Ideology: Example and Ideas                      87

6
Institutional Reform                            115

Bibliography                                     131
Name Index                                       143
Subject Index                                    145

# Preface

This book is based on my Ohlin Lectures, delivered at the Stockholm School of Economics in October 1987. Needless to say, not all that is included here was read on the occasion, even though I come from the "fluent society"—India—and was introduced to the audience by Professor Staffan Burenstam Linder as the "fastest tongue in the East."

In writing and rewriting the lectures, I profited from the ideas and criticisms of many friends in the large community of scholars in international economics. I would be remiss if, despite the risk of offending others through omission, I did not thank the following: David Baldwin, Robert Baldwin, Magnus Blomström, Richard Brecher, Barry Eichengreen, Michael Finger, Elhanan Helpman, Gene Grossman, Brian Hindley, Isaiah Frank, Charles Kindleberger, Anne Krueger, Sam Laird, Robert Lawrence, Assar Lindbeck, Mats Lundahl, Alasdair MacBean, Steve Marks, Patrick Messerlin, Helen Milner, Douglas Nelson, Sarath Rajapatirana, John Ruggie, Richard Snape, T. N. Srinivasan, Aaron Tornell, and Tom Willett. The research assistance of Brian Wesol was a great help to me.

I must also mention with pleasure my Columbia student Douglas Irwin, who helped with the tedious research and who provided intellectual energy and input wholly disproportionate to his youth. I am greatly indebted to him.

# Introduction

I first encountered Bertil Ohlin at Brissago in 1958, at an international conference organized by Roy Harrod. Strikingly handsome, austerely elegant, he seemed a formidable figure, stepping out of a distant and glorious Swedish past that had also given us Knut Wicksell and Eli Heckscher. Even in that splendid company, he stood tall. He was one of those rare people who distinguish themselves in both science and practical affairs—he had successfully made a transition from eminence in economics to prominence in politics. The leader of Sweden's Liberal Party for more than two decades and the Minister of Trade from 1944 to 1945, he had already written by 1933 the celebrated work *Interregional and International Trade,* for which he later earned the Nobel Memorial Prize.

But anyone who might have feared that distinction had bred distance and made Bertil Ohlin unapproachable would have been in for a surprise. He was remarkably affable. And anyone who might have expected his absence from the academic world since his election to the Swedish Parliament (in 1938) to have dulled his intellect or stilled his curiosity was manifestly in error. I was struck by the evident ease with which he held his own in economic discourse with such luminaries as Gottfried Haberler and Harry Johnson. Years later, the distinguished economist Göran Ohlin (his nephew) told me that when television had arrived on the Swedish scene, Bertil Ohlin had been widely regarded as certain to benefit politically because of his fetching good looks, but that his fierce intellect had insistently gotten in the way. Substance, to which the new medium was no friend, was central to Bertil Ohlin's being.

Nothing would be more apt than to celebrate his memory by addressing a present-day issue that would have engaged both his interests and his intellect. Protectionism is such an issue.

After twenty-five years of successful postwar trade liberalization in the developed countries, during which round after round of negotiations under the auspices of the General Agreement on Tariffs and Trade had slashed tariffs to unprecedented lows, the threat of protectionism has resurfaced. Today's parliaments and congresses, negotiating forums, and economic summits bear agonizing witness to the efforts to stem the tide of protectionist sentiments and legislation. It is necessary, however, to rise above the daily din of these battles and examine the underlying trends that will shape the world's trading arrangements as we approach the twenty-first century.

Interests and ideology interact to shape these underlying trends. My major theme will be that contrapuntal tendencies can be distinguished in interests and in ideology, and that the deck is not stacked in favor of protectionism. Contrary to what the current difficulties suggest, there are major new interests and forces, prompted particularly by the growing globalization and interdependence in the world economy, that offer grounds for guarded optimism. Equally, there are new ideas in the theory of commercial policy, chiefly resulting from the new developments in the theory of political economy, that strengthen the ideological force of anti-protectionism.

However, to assist the hand of history, so that it does not falter, we will have to reform and strengthen the institutional framework, national and international, to harness these pro-trade interests and contain the forces of protectionism more effectively. The trading system is vulnerable to protectionism, but it also offers new opportunities to combat it. These opportunities must be seized by means of bold, imaginative, and perhaps difficult institutional changes.

# Protectionism

# Postwar Liberalization

A backward glance at the postwar years of trade liberalization by the industrialized countries, and at the resurgence of protectionism since the 1970s, offers valuable insights into the historical interplay of interests, ideology, and institutional structure that shaped trade policies, and thus prepares the way for the analysis of future developments.

The Bretton Woods conference, held in 1944, had designed an institutional infrastructure that embodied the principles of a liberal international economic order. Adherence to the rules of the International Monetary Fund would provide macroeconomic equilibrium, without which the maintenance of a liberal trading system is economically less compelling and politically more difficult. The General Agreement on Tariffs and Trade provided rules—reflecting multilateralism and nondiscrimination—that would enable the contracting parties to reap gains from trade according to the principles of the theory of comparative advantage.[1] The institutional *troika* also included the World Bank, which was designed to channel resources to the developing nations in order to strengthen

1. The International Trade Organization, not GATT, was the original trade organization devised at Bretton Woods. It never got off the ground, however.

the liberal infrastructure (which would otherwise have been long on the market and short on sentiment).

The United States, which emerged as the dominant world power after World War II, is generally credited with the evolution of this Benthamite infrastructure for the world economy. The conception was not all American: the role of John Maynard Keynes was pivotal.[2] Indeed, the British view of the matter is conveyed with the characteristic arrogance of the metropolitan elite towards the ex-colonial *nouveau riche* in the doggerel:

*In Washington Lord Halifax*
*Once whispered to Lord Keynes:*
*It's true* they *have the money bags*
*But* we *have all the brains.*

But evidently the United States played the dominant role, if not in the design then in the propagation and sustenance of this infrastructure. As the major power on the world economic and political scene, it provided the ideology and the political and material support for the new international economic regime. A *Pax Americana* had succeeded the *Pax Britannica* of the nineteenth century.

The question as to why the United States threw its weight behind a liberal trading order is an interesting one. It bears directly on the central question of how interests and ideology influence the present and the future course of pro-

2. Keynes had also planned a commodity-stabilization scheme, with an institution to be called COMMOD. His memorandum on the subject has been published in the *Journal of International Economics* (1974). This institution has not materialized, though concerns regarding volatility in commodity prices are mirrored in the efforts of developing countries at the United Nations Conference on Trade and Development (UNCTAD) and elsewhere to promote commodity-stabilization schemes. Neither Keynes nor anyone else at the time seems to have anticipated the need to make corresponding institutional arrangements, as part of the international infrastructure, to oversee labor migrations across borders.

tectionism in the world economy. But before tackling it, let us review the remarkable consequences of the liberal trading order.

## Liberalization and Its Consequences

GATT did not eliminate trade restrictions in one fell swoop; it was an umbrella under which a series of tariff-cutting exercises were undertaken. The process of tariff reduction was spread over seven rounds (not counting the ongoing Uruguay Round, launched in September 1986). In the United States, the average tariff declined by nearly 92 percent over the 33 years spanned by the Geneva Round of 1947 and the Tokyo Round (figure 1). By the early 1980s, the tariff level had gone down to 4.9 percent in the United States, 6.0 percent in the European Economic Community, and 5.4 percent in Japan.[3]

Tariff reduction evidently continued beyond the 1973 success of the Organization of Petroleum Exporting Countries and the difficulties that followed in the remainder of the 1970s. However, the growth of nontariff barriers in the 1970s and the 1980s offset the liberalization of trade that tariff reductions implied. Thus, the unprecedented growth of trade and income that accompanied trade liberalization is evident only until the early 1970s.

From 1953 to 1963, world income grew at an annual rate of 4.3 percent and world trade at a rate of 6.1 percent. For the period 1963 to 1973, the performance was even more dramatic: 5.1 percent and 8.9 percent, respectively (figure 2). This remarkable performance was dominated by the industri-

---

3. These are the estimated average tariff rates after the Tokyo Round (1974–1979) cuts are fully implemented. See *World Development Report* 1987, figure 8.1.

---

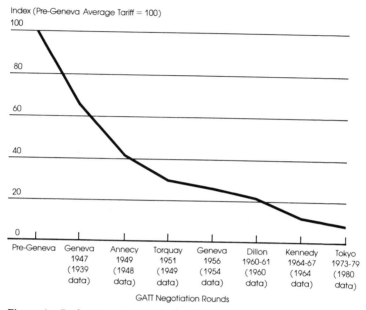

Index (Pre-Geneva Average Tariff = 100)

GATT Negotiation Rounds

Figure 1   Reductions in average U.S. tariff rates after GATT rounds. Indexes are calculated from percentage reductions in average weighted tariff rates given in Finger 1979 (table 1, page 425) and World Bank 1987 (table 8.1, page 136). Weighted average U.S. tariff rate after Tokyo Round was 4.6 percent (World Bank 1987).

alized countries (figure 3), whose share of world exports was 71.0 percent in 1960.[4]

Did the trade liberalization cause the trade expansion, and did that, in turn, produce the economic prosperity of the 1950s and the 1960s? The fact that trade grew significantly more rapidly than income (figures 2 and 3) is certainly suggestive. The extra edge could well have been due to the steady dismantling of the trade barriers; in fact, it would be astonishing if that were not the case. But the link between trade and income growth is more complex. Did rapid income

4. As late as 1980 it was 66.1%, as calculated from the *International Financial Statistics* (International Monetary Fund 1985, pp. 108–109).

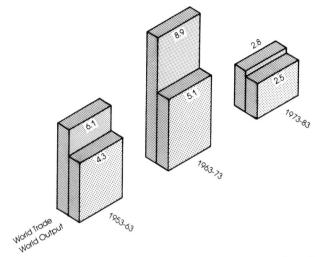

Figure 2   Average annual growth rates (in percent) of world trade and world output for the periods 1953–1963, 1963–1973, and 1973–1983. Source: Hufbauer and Schott 1985, table A-1, page 97.

growth lead to rapid trade expansion, or was it the other way around? I suspect that, as with most economic phenomena, there was a genuine two-way relationship.

## From Growth to Trade

An increase in income generally leads to a corresponding expansion of trade, unless the pattern of growth-induced supply and corresponding demands is such as to create an anti-trade bias.[5] In fact, with the trade expansion being focused largely on the industrialized countries, the effect is rather likely to have been characterized by a pro-trade bias. As Staffan Burenstam Linder argued in his seminal 1961 book, intra-industry trade in similar products (for example, small cars

5. This terminology was introduced in the 1950s in the theoretical literature on growth and trade that followed concerns with the "dollar shortage" and the hypothesis that relatively faster U.S. growth and productivity change were responsible for it. See Johnson 1955.

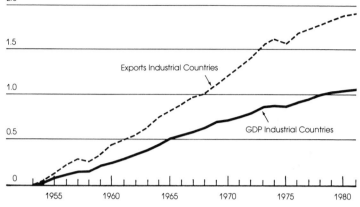

Figure 3  Growth of industrial countries' exports and gross domestic product in the period 1953–1981, based on International Monetary Fund indexes. Sources: International Monetary Fund 1982; International Monetary Fund 1985.

and large cars) is an important characteristic of trade among the industrialized countries. This alone could imply a higher rather than a lower ratio of trade to gross national product as incomes increase and consumption gets increasingly more diversified in terms of variety within broad industry groups while the trading countries continue to specialize in production of similar goods with differentiated characteristics.

At the same time, such intra-industry trade undoubtedly lessened the political costs of trade liberalization and thereby facilitated the process of tariff reduction in the postwar period. If industries have to contract when trade barriers are reduced, resistance to liberalization can be expected; however, if the outcome is more specialization within industries, so that they give up on certain products and increase the manufacture of others, the resistance to liberalization will surely be less.

The evidence confirms that the effect of postwar liberalization and income growth in the industrialized countries was indeed to increase intra-industry specialization rather than inter-industry specialization. In an important study of the European Economic Community, Bela Balassa (1975) analyzed the expansion of intra-EEC trade during the periods 1958–1963 and 1958–1970 and documented the increasing similarity in the pattern of manufactured-goods exports among the EEC countries.[6]

But if intra-industry trade reduced the political costs of tariff cuts, thus easing their progress and contributing to growing shares of trade in national income, so did growing incomes. It is obvious but necessary to recall that, all else being equal, a growing economy reduces the need to contract industries in response to trade liberalization. A mere slow-down in the rate of growth in an industry losing to foreign competition, rather than an absolute decline with its attendant losses and layoffs, can be a pleasing consequence of a growing economy. If tariff cuts lead to more trade, and more trade produces more income, and more income facilitates more tariff cuts, the result is a "virtuous circle" that can produce the level of prosperity we saw in the glorious 1950s and 1960s.

## From Trade to Growth

It is plausible that liberalization-induced trade expansion, through its efficiency effects (called in jargon the "gains from trade"), fed the postwar growth of incomes. Now, it is indeed possible to construct theoretical cases in which, para-doxically, the effect of trade liberalization on growth is perverse. Imagine that liberalization shifts the distribution of income in favor of groups that save less. Then, if the national savings rate is determined not by fiscal policy but by the

6. See Balassa 1975, pp. 108–110, for details.

market-determined distribution of income, the liberalization will improve current income but may reduce its rate of growth (which reflects not just current productivity but also the rate of savings and investment).[7] But surely there is no reason to consider such paradoxes relevant to the broad postwar experience.

Nor need one be bothered by the occasional argument that trade liberalization brings a one-time-only gain in income rather than a sustained improvement in growth.[8] A substantial trade liberalization could spread a one-time-only effect over two decades. Besides, there have been repeated tariff cuts through the many rounds (recall figure 1), so a favorable effect on growth rates could have been repeated, and thus sustained, through an extended period without any difficulty.

But what is one to make of the contention that growth rates can reflect a host of factors other than trade liberalization (including, in the European case, a "catching-up" or "recovery" phenomenon that might accelerate growth back to pre–World War II rates)? Indeed, few phenomena in economics can be explained by reference to single causes. But this does not rule out the possibility, and indeed the overwhelming probability, that diminishing trade barriers were a major contributory force in the postwar expansion of incomes. It would be a *non sequitur* to argue that, because other fac-

7. For a discussion of this possibility, see Bhagwati 1968. For a careful, analytical demonstration, see Pattanaik 1974. See Corden 1971 for a more comprehensive analysis of the effect of trade on the rate of growth, and Findlay 1984 for an elegant and complete analytical model addressed to this issue.

8. This argument is not valid in the Harrod-Domar model, where an improved productivity of resources will permanently improve the growth rate, given the savings rate. In the Cobb-Douglas model, however, the growth rate cannot be permanently improved by a one-time-only improvement in productivity. See Solow 1956.

tors also influenced growth, trade liberalization could not have done so. In fact, several empirical analyses of time-series data for specific countries—analyses in which other contributory factors have been controlled for in principle—have underscored the link between trade liberalization and improved export performance (and, hence, enhanced economic performance).[9]

## Exceptions to Liberalization

There have been some important exceptions to the trend toward liberalization. Some of them were present from the outset; others arose as the postwar period unfolded.

### Agriculture

Exempted from most of GATT's discipline,[10] agriculture suffered yet further from the 1955 waiver granted to the United States, and from its spread thereafter (a historical fact that seems somewhat ironic today, in view of U.S. conversion on this issue). There was hardly any support for the inclusion of

9. This evidence, for many semi-industrialized developing countries, was accumulated in massive research projects undertaken in the 1960s and 1970s at the Organization for Economic Cooperation and Development, the World Bank, the National Bureau of Economic Research, and the Kiel Institute of Development Economics. These and other findings, and the explanations of the link noted above, are reviewed in Bhagwati 1985c, 1986c and in Balassa 1986. I admit, however, to sharing the view that cross-section evidence on the question is less persuasive, since one cannot meaningfully control for several factors that may differentially affect the growth of the countries in the sample. Thus, it does not really make sense, no matter how good your $R^2$, to infer a link between trade liberalization and growth rates by putting on one regression line countries with totally different savings rates, foreign investment, shares of public in total investment, and so forth.

10. Loopholes for agriculture were written into Articles XI and XVI from the start.

agriculture on the liberalization agenda, because the United States and the major developed countries of Europe were generally captive to strong protectionist lobbies that had constructed elaborate mechanisms of agricultural income support. At the same time, the major developing countries were protecting their manufactures instead and therefore were not interested in lobbying for agricultural trade liberalization.[11] If I may paint with a very broad brush, the postwar period found the developed countries stoutly protecting their agriculture while steadily dismantling protection for their manufactures, while the developing countries protected their manufactures through a combination of trade and exchange restrictions and therefore (inadvertently) created disincentives for their agriculture. The political preference for "agriculturalization" in the developed countries was matched by that for "industrialization" in the developing countries. (Eventually the United States—perceiving its comparative advantage in agricultural trade—lent its immense weight to the inclusion of agriculture on the agenda of the Uruguay Round.)

But the major exceptions to trade liberalization, which manifested themselves as the process unfolded and which (in hindsight) turn out to have been indicative of the protectionist problems that would surface more clearly in the 1970s, lay elsewhere. Today's "systemic" threats to freer trade are the persistent use of nontariff barriers to meet sectoral difficulties in the developed countries and the pervasive and sustained use of trade and exchange restrictions to manage the balance of payments and to protect domestic industries in the developing countries. Both problems became manifest early on.

11. I doubt that even a strong desire for agricultural trade liberalization by the major developing countries would have made much difference in the early postwar years, given their relatively small role in overall world trade and their low political profile and clout.

## Textiles

The proliferation of nontariff barriers was presaged by efforts to organize trade in textiles. In 1961 the United States, under pressure from the domestic industry, managed to get the Short-Term Cotton Textile Arrangement negotiated. That arrangement led, in the following year, to the Long-Term Arrangement Regarding International Trade in Textiles, which consisted, in essence, of a series of bilateral agreements under which import quotas were fixed by source, thus sanctifying the use of voluntary export restrictions (bilateral quotas mutually agreed upon and assigned to specific exporting countries). Since such arrangements inherently discriminate among supply sources, getting them negotiated under GATT—which strongly affirms the nondiscriminatory most-favored-nation principle—was like getting the pope to preside over a pagan rite.

GATT also compromises on the most-favored-nation principle in dealing with the question of integration. Article XXIV legitimates the formation of customs unions and free-trade areas and permits member countries to join these arrangements to cut tariffs for one another but not for other member countries, thus denying the latter the benefit of their most-favored-nation rights. In practice, Article XXIV has been invoked with even more latitude than was originally conceived, reflecting accommodation to the political objectives of powerful GATT members. The United States, broadly sympathizing with the political objectives and implications of European integration, threw its weight behind a relaxed interpretation of Article XXIV when the European Economic Community was formed.[12] But in view of its conviction that the most-favored-nation (MFN) principle was valuable, the United States abstained from resorting to Arti-

12. See Jackson 1969, p. 589.

cle XXIV, preferring multilateral MFN-based trade liberalization through the 1970s. However, in the 1980s, the United States, in a more wide-ranging reversal of its pro-MFN attitudes and policies, turned to Article XXIV to initiate a yet looser free-trade area with Israel and to work toward a similar preferential arrangement with Canada.

## The Developing Countries

But whereas these acts of omission (agriculture) and commission (the Long-Term Arrangement in textiles and other exceptions to MFN-based multilateralism) were due to political pressures from the powerful, the ability of the developing countries to virtually escape symmetric GATT obligations of access to their own markets by others was due to their weakness.

The economic theories and ideological predilections that led the developing countries toward extensive protection and the associated import-substitution programs were undoubtedly important, and I will describe them presently. But their ability to get GATT to accommodate to the resulting situation by adopting the doctrine of *special and differential treatment,* under which the member developing countries would enjoy the benefits of increasing market access abroad while being exempted from having to offer greater access to their own markets,[13] was surely due to their unimportance in trade rather than their political strength in negotiations. The demands of these countries could, in consequence, be accommodated, fraying the liberal trading regime only at the margin while securing a large and growing membership of the institution that embodied the principles of the liberal or-

13. Special and Differential treatment also extends to the different question of preferential treatment of the developing countries in their access to the markets of the developed countries. Part IV of GATT was introduced largely to legitimate schemes giving such preferences.

der. At the same time, the relative economic insignificance of these countries in world trade implied that the "cost" to others of their asymmetric escape from the process of liberalization was small enough to warrant neglect and invite indulgence.

The consequence of this asymmetry was that the developing countries, a growing political and economic reality through the postwar period, generally exhibited high trends of protection throughout this period.[14] These levels of protection appear to have been high relative to those calculated for several currently developed countries in the early twentieth century, as table 1 shows.[15] They were certainly higher than the protection levels of the developed countries—a situation that would continue even with the offsetting growth of nontariff barriers in the developed countries during the 1970s and recently. Indeed, by recent UN Conference on Trade and Development estimates, in 1986 the developing countries seemed (in percentage of items affected by such nontariff barriers) to outperform the developed countries quite handsomely in virtually all classes of imports, including agricultural materials, ores and metals, and manufactures.[16]

Warts and all, however, the postwar trade liberalization was a major accomplishment. What brought it about?

14. Among the more important documentations of the high protection levels in major developing countries during the 1950s and 1960s is Balassa 1971.

15. This conclusion needs some qualification insofar as the "natural" protection found in the earlier periods would be greater because of higher transport costs. Note, however, that the table considers only tariff rates, whereas import quotas have been substantially more important in the developing countries in the postwar period.

16. The overall estimate of this incidence was more than 3 times as high for the developing countries as for the developed countries, as figure 4 shows. This asymmetry of trade barriers among the two blocs of countries is illuminatingly documented in Laird and Finger's (1986) study, which is based on documentation produced under the auspices of the International Bank for Reconstruction and Development (i.e. the World Bank) and UNCTAD.

# Table 1

Estimates of nominal tariff levels for manufactures (percent). Source: Little et al. 1970, table 5.1.

|  | 1902 | 1913 | 1925 |  |
|---|---|---|---|---|
| *Developed and European Countries* | | | | |
| Russia | 131 | | | |
| Spain | 76 | 41 | 41 | |
| United States | 73 | 44 | 37 | 11.5 (1962) |
| Portugal | 71 | | | |
| France | 34 | 20 | 21 | |
| Italy | 27 | 18 | 22 | |
| Germany | 25 | 13 | 20 | |
| Sweden | 23 | 20 | 16 | 6.6 (1962) |
| Denmark | 18 | 14 | 10 | |
| Canada | 17 | 26 | 23 | |
| Belgium | 13 | 9 | 15 | |
| Norway | 12 | | | |
| New Zealand | 9 | | | |
| Japan | 9 | | | 16.1 (1962) |
| Switzerland | 7 | 9 | 14 | |
| Australia | 6 | 16 | 27 | |
| Netherlands | 3 | 4 | 6 | |
| European Economic Community | | | | 11.0 (1962) |
| *Developing Countries* | | | | |
| Argentina | 28 | 28 | 29 | 141 (1958) |
| Brazil | | | | 99 (1966) |
| Mexico | | | | 22 (1960) |
| British India | 3 | 4 | 16 | |
| Pakistan | | | | 93 (1963/4) |
| Philippines | | | | 46 (1961) |
| Taiwan | | | | 30 (1966) |

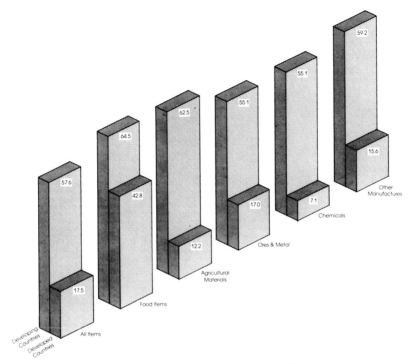

Figure 4 Percentage of items affected by nontariff measures (including quotas, prohibitions, restrictive exchange allocations, other financial requirements, price-control measures, automatic licensing, and technical requirements) applied by fifty developing countries and fifteen major developed countries in 1986. (If two measures affect an item, only the items affected are counted, irrespective of the number of measures they face. Items are covered at the four-digit CCCN level. The percentages measure the items affected as a proportion of all possible items.) Source: UNCTAD 1987.

# Ideology, Interests, and Institutions

# 2

Profound commitments to policies are generally due to a mix of ideological factors (in the form of ideas and example), interests (as defined by politics and economics), and institutions (as they shape constraints and opportunities).

Few economists have seriously doubted the significance of the influence of ideas on policy since Keynes wrote: "The ideas of economists and political philosophers, both when they are right and when they are wrong, are more powerful than is commonly understood. Indeed, the world is ruled by little else. Practical men, who believe themselves to be quite exempt from any intellectual influence, are usually the slaves of some defunct economist." (1936, p. 383) Those who continue to doubt this ought to heed the greater eloquence of Thomas Carlyle. His loquacity at a dinner led a companion to reproach him: "Ideas, Mr. Carlyle, ideas, nothing but ideas!" Carlyle retorted: "There was once a man called Rousseau who wrote a book containing nothing but ideas. The second edition was bound in the skins of those who laughed at the first." (See MacIntyre 1985.)

But ideas play on a stage where interests are no less in evidence. It would be vulgar to claim that interests dominate exclusively, the appropriate ideology being chosen simply to legitimate the triumphant interests. However, John Stuart Mill surely had it right when he observed that "a good cause seldom triumphs unless someone's interest is bound up in it."[1]

This interplay of interests and ideology is nowhere more evident than in the episode of the repeal of the Corn Laws, which occurred in 1846 and which ushered in Britain's nineteenth-century embrace of free trade. This historic transition was neither exclusively the result of interests nor entirely the product of a powerful ideology.

Although Richard Cobden's rhetoric and his vision were inspired by faith in the economic and political merits of free trade for Britain, and indeed for the trading world at large, his Anti–Corn Law League drew much of its support from the fact that cheap corn imports were seen as profitable for consumers and for industry. This created ample "sectional-interest," pressure-group support for Cobden's "social-interest"-inspired movement. In the end, however, the repeal of the Corn Laws turned on Prime Minister Robert Peel's cerebral conversion to the idea of free trade, which led him to abandon the sectional protectionist interests of his Conservative Party. Indeed, charged by his foe Disraeli with having betrayed his party for the principles of political economy, Peel found his political career destroyed beyond repair.[2]

1. Quoted in Kindleberger's (1982–83) insightful examination of historical cycles in protection and free trade.

2. Sarah Bradford, in her biography of Disraeli, observes: "To [the Conservatives] Peel, in twice reversing his position on two great issues of the day, Catholic Emancipation and the Corn Laws, was guilty of betraying his party and the principles upon which he had come to power. It was this view, which concerned not economics but party principle, that Disraeli hammered home so successfully, and it was this same general feeling among parliamentarians of both sides that was primarily responsible for Peel's fall" (1984, p. 159). She cites a contemporary's telling remark: "[Peel] cared a great deal, he saw so much clearly, and yet at some points he was shut in by political economy as if by a fog."

PAPA COBDEN TAKING MASTER ROBERT A FREE TRADE WALK.

PAPA COBDEN.—"Come along, MASTER ROBERT, do step out."
MASTER ROBERT.—"That's all very well, but you know I cannot go so fast as you do."

This 1845 cartoon from *Punch* shows Cobden leading Peel toward
free trade, underlining Cobden's advocacy and Peel's later
conversion.

Peel was "persuaded, not purchased; baptised, not bought."[3]

The remarkable role played by Peel also illustrates well the opportunity provided by the parliamentary structure of British politics and the relatively elitist nature of the politics of the time. These factors facilitated an ideologically converted prime minister's ability to get around the special interests within his party.

Similarly, the postwar liberalization of trade can be explained in terms of forces that span ideas and example, interests and institutions.

---

## Example

The architects of the liberal postwar order and the ensuing trade liberalization were not merely intellectual believers in the virtues of freer trade. They were also the beneficiaries of a splendid historical example: an experience with tariffs that was widely perceived to have been a spectacular failure.

The Great Depression had been associated with beggar-my-neighbor policies of competitive exchange-rate depreciation and tariff escalation, each aimed at preserving and deflecting aggregate demand toward one's own industries at the expense of those of one's trading partners.[4] Few believe

3. Bhagwati and Irwin 1987, p. 130. Peel's own papers record his change of opinion on this issue of free trade. Parker (1899, p. 220) writes: "[Peel] had removed prohibitory duties on foreign cattle and meat, and had lowered duties on sugar and on other articles of food. . . . Of himself Sir Robert Peel writes, 'The opinions I had previously entertained had undergone a great change.' " Peel is also on record as saying: "I will not withhold the damage which is due to the progress of reason and to truth, by denying that my opinions on the subject of protection have undergone a change" (Gash 1972, p. 567).

4. The Smoot-Hawley tariff of 1930 in the U.S., which I discuss below, was characterized by some new duties that could not be explained by conventional protective reasons but were evidently aimed at diverting demand

Representative Willis Hawley (R, Oregon) and Senator Reed Smoot (R, Utah) at the U.S. Capitol, April 11, 1929.

that such policies caused the Depression; there are many more plausible candidates for the role of villain.[5] But it is certainly arguable that the tariff escalations deepened the Depression.[6]

away from foreign goods. Mann (1987) cites Isaacs' (1948) study on this question, including the example of a 1000% increase in the tariff on cashew nuts (not produced in the U.S. then). The fact that the U.S. was also running a balance-of-payments surplus at the time made these duties particularly irksome as evidence of beggar-my-neighbor policies unworthy of a creditor nation. Mann quotes Liepmann (1938): "Nothing has contributed more to the impeding of international trade relations than the American tariff of 1930, by which the greatest creditor nation in the world surrounded itself at the moment of severe crises with the highest tariff walls in its history."

5. See, for instance, the rival explanations of Friedman and Schwartz (1963), Kindleberger (1986), and Temin (1976).

6. However, as Eichengreen (1986) has suggested, the evidence can be analyzed as indicating (mildly) otherwise for the U.S. in the case of the Smoot-Hawley tariff.

In any event, the *perception* grew and persisted that the Smoot-Hawley tariff-raising binge, in which virtually every industry was rewarded with its own "made-to-order" tariff[7] (with the apparent consequence of foreign tariff retaliations[8] and a worsening depression), was a disaster.

As John Kenneth Galbraith has wittily said of an economist foe, his misfortune has been that his theories have been applied: blooming in the ivory tower, they have wilted in the real world. For the proponents of free trade, the magnitude of the failure of tariffs, and indeed of their seemingly counterproductive results, during the Depression was a real dividend. It helped to stack the cards in favor of the pro-trade forces, providing the ideological momentum for liberal trade that persists to this date.[9]

Whereas this pro-trade bias was shared by all the countries that the Depression afflicted, its principal convert was the United States.[10] This would be critical, as the United States was steadily emerging as a major force and the Second World War would leave it as the dominant power shaping the world economy. The immediate result, even before the war, was a dramatic (indeed drastic) shift in trade policy by a chastened group of American policymakers.

---

7. Schattschneider's (1935) account of the enactment of the Smoot-Hawley tariff is one of the great turning points in the theory of political economy. Incidentally, the tariff should have been called Hawley-Smoot, since a bill is customarily named after its first proposer in the process and since a tariff (being a revenue bill) has to originate in the House and then go to the Senate. But fame, like infamy, evidently does not play by protocol.

8. Eichengreen (1986) cites some tentative evidence that the tariffs enacted later by Canada and some European countries were due to the Depression and might have arisen even if there had been no Smoot-Hawley tariff to retaliate against.

9. Goldstein (1986) has used the phrase "liberal bias" to describe this ideological shift.

10. This was natural. After all, the U.S.-legislated Smoot-Hawley tariff had been the most visible and dramatic act of anti-trade folly.

---

The institutional structure that had facilitated the enactment of the Smoot-Hawley tariff was modified. Stung by its own failure and by a severe electoral judgment, the Congress—which had given in to each sectional interest's demand for tariff protection—acquiesced in a classic shift of power in trade-policy initiatives and management to the executive branch, which was less amenable to constituency pressure. This was coupled with an active, negotiated dismantling of the post-depression tariff walls under the 1934 Reciprocal Trade Agreements Act by an executive branch that was not only freer from protectionist constituency pressures (directly and indirectly via the Congress) but also eager to indulge the newly acquired pro-trade bias.[11] The pro-trade bias would also underlie the institutional design of GATT at the end of the war.[12]

## Ideas

The pro-trade bias, strengthened by the interwar experience of competitive and retaliatory tariff-making, lay comfortably within the intellectual tradition of free trade that had existed

11. There is an important dispute among the students of U.S. trade policy as to whether the pro-trade bias was only in the executive branch or also extended to Congress in the postwar period. The conventional view, stated by Pastor (1983) and shared by many political scientists, is that Congress was to become equally infected by this pro-trade bias and indulged in constituency-directed protectionist noises while getting the executive branch to nip actual protectionism in the bud. This "cry-and-sigh syndrome" thesis has been challenged by Nelson (1987), who argues that Congress has continued to reflect constituency pressures but that its ability to deliver protection has been reduced by the institutional shift toward administered protection and by the pro-trade bias of the executive branch.

12. GATT was not the original institution designed at the Bretton Woods Conference in 1944. Rather, the International Trade Organization had been proposed, along with the IMF and the World Bank. However, the ITO was not ratified, and GATT—intended only to be a transitional agreement— became the de facto institution overseeing trade in the postwar period.

since the time of Adam Smith. But it is critical to understand just how.

## The Intellectual Case for Unilateral Free Trade

The theory of commercial policy, as it evolved from David Ricardo and John Stuart Mill through the writings of Alfred Marshall and Francis Edgeworth at the turn of the nineteenth century, strongly implied that a nation would profit most by pursuing a free trade policy and that this was so whether its trading partners were free-traders or protectionists. *Unilateral* free trade emerged as the prescription from this corpus of thought.

### The Theory

Central to this theory was the notion that—given external trading opportunities—specialization and the ensuing exchange would ensure gains from trade among nations engaged in voluntary transactions. It is easy enough to see this today, but when the early economists propagated this notion it was in contradiction to the dominant doctrine of mercantilism. The virtues of division of labor and exchange, noted even in Plato's *Republic*,[13] had been lost to oblivion. Mercantilism and its legitimation of autarkic protective policies seemed to be only common sense, reminding one that common sense is what makes a person assert that the earth is flat, for that is how it appears to the naked eye.

The new science of political economy focused on trade as an opportunity to specialize in production, to exchange what one produced efficiently for what others produced efficiently, and thus to wind up with more rather than less. A policy of

13. I stumbled on Plato's remarkable statement of the advantages of specialization, found that it was indeed a lost treasure, and had George Stigler (the Nobel laureate and distinguished connoisseur of intellectual history in economics) publish it on the back cover of the *Journal of Political Economy* in 1985.

free trade would guide a nation to an efficient utilization of this trade opportunity. In essence, as postwar theorists of international trade would clarify, free trade would maximize returns by efficiently utilizing two alternative ways of securing any good: through specialized production of other goods, to be exchanged in trade for the desired good, and through domestic production of the desired good. Free trade would ensure that these two alternative techniques—trade and domestic production—would be used efficiently (that is, in such a mix as to produce equal returns at the margin). (For a formal statement of these theoretical principles, see chapter 17 of Bhagwati and Srinivasan 1983.)

Two critical assumptions underlay this neat conclusion, and the classical economists were cognizant of them in their own way.

The first was that free trade would guide one to the efficient outcome only if the price mechanism worked well. Prices had to reflect true social costs. John Stuart Mill was smart enough to warn that the protection of infant industries could be justified. In modern language: If there were future returns that could not be captured by an infant industry but would dissipate to others in the country, this market failure justified protection.

Equally, if a country's trade in a sector was large enough to confer on it the ability to affect prices, then a tariff could enable the country to restrict its trade and gain more (just as a monopolist can increase profits by restricting his sales). Hence, this came to be known as the *monopoly-power-in-trade* argument for protection.

The second assumption was that a country's external trade opportunity had to be independent of its own trade policy. Suppose that, by imposing tariffs, you could pry open the protected markets of your trading partners. That could conceivably justify the use of tariffs, in which case unilateral free trade would not be desirable. Even Adam Smith was aware of this possible qualification; indeed, he considered the question at some length:

*The case in which it may sometimes be a matter of deliberation how far it is proper to continue the free importation of certain foreign goods, is, when some foreign nation restrains by high duties or prohibitions the importation of some of our manufactures into their country. Revenge in this case naturally dictates retaliation, and that we should impose the like duties and prohibitions upon the importation of some or all of their manufactures into ours. Nations accordingly seldom fail to retaliate in the manner.*

*There may be good policy in retaliations of this kind, when there is a probability that they will procure the repeal of the high duties or prohibitions complained of. The recovery of a great foreign market will generally more than compensate the transitory inconveniencey of paying dearer during a short time for some sorts of goods. To judge whether such retaliations are likely to produce such an effect, does not, perhaps, belong so much to the science of a legislator, whose deliberations ought to be governed by general principles which are always the same, as to the skill of that insidious and crafty animal, vulgarly called a stateman or politician, whose councils are directed by the momentary fluctuations of affairs. When there is no probability that any such repeal can be procured, it seems a bad method of compensating the injury done to certain classes of our people, to do another injury ourselves, not only to those classes, but to almost all the other classes of them. (1776, pp. 434–435)*

Smith's skepticism toward retaliatory protection was later to be shared by the great British economist Alfred Marshall and by others who recognized its theoretical possibility but nonetheless advocated unilateral free trade in practice.

*Empirical Judgment and the Nineteenth-Century British Debate*
In the end, the intellectual case for free trade and the case for free trade as a unilateral policy had to rest on the empirical

judgment that the exceptions were unimportant or were merely theoretical *curiosa,* and that, even if this were not so, protectionist policies based on them were likely to cause more harm than good.

This is evident from the remarkable debate that ensued at the end of the nineteenth century when Britain, in relative decline as Germany and the United States rose in economic stature, found its long-standing policy of unilateral free trade in serious jeopardy from the "reciprocitarians," who wanted Britain to match the tariffs of other countries with tariffs of her own. British statesmen and economists who were wedded to unilateralism marshaled the following arguments against the reciprocitarians[14]:

• The belief in the folly of protection was so complete that it was felt that grievous losses to be suffered by its practitioners would suffice to induce them to embrace free trade. The *Times* editorialized in 1881 that "protection, as we well know, brings its own punishment. We are safe, therefore, in leaving its adherents to the stern teaching of facts. Nature will retaliate upon France whether we do so or not."

• Others believed that the success of a free-trading Britain would make her an example for other nations. In 1846 Robert Peel had argued in Parliament, in defense of a unilateral free-trade policy, that

*If other countries choose to buy in the dearest market, such an option on their part constitutes no reason why we should not be permitted to buy in the cheapest. I trust the Government . . . will not resume the policy which they and we have found most inconvenient, namely, the haggling with foreign countries about reciprocal concessions, instead of taking that independent course which we believe to be conducive to our own interests. Let us trust to the influence of public*

14. For a more extensive discussion see Bhagwati and Irwin 1987.

**THE BRITISH LION IN 1850;**

OR, THE EFFECTS OF FREE TRADE.

This 1846 cartoon from *Punch*, showing the British lion in plenitude and prosperity after the repeal of the Corn Laws, illustrates the supreme confidence that the supporters of free trade had in its virtues.

*opinion in other countries—let us trust that our example, with the proof of practical benefits we derive from it, will at no remote period insure the adoption of the principles on which we have acted.*

• Richard Cobden, the great crusader for the repeal of the Corn Laws and the adoption of free trade, went so far as to argue that insisting on reciprocal tariff reductions would only make the task of free-traders abroad more difficult by implying that free trade was really in Britain's interest rather than their own. Thus, the Anti–Corn Law League emphasized Britain's potential gain from a free trade policy but "expressly refrained from appealing to any foreign sentiment in favour of the [free trade] cause [, for] they rightly judged that such appeals were certain to be misrepresented by the interests which stood behind protective tariffs and would play into the hands of their enemies" (Hobson 1919, p. 40). As Cobden put it,

*We came to the conclusion that the less we attempted to persuade foreigners to adopt our trade principles, the better; for we discovered so much suspicion of the motives of England, that it was lending an argument to the protectionists abroad to incite the popular feeling against free-traders, by enabling them to say, "See what these men are wanting to do; they are partisans of England and they are seeking to prostitute our industries at the feet of that perfidious nation. . . ." To take away this pretense, we avowed our total indifference whether other nations became free-traders or not; but we should abolish Protection for our own selves, and leave other countries to take whatever course they liked best.[15] (quoted in Hobson 1919, p. 41)*

15. That many thought Britain would gain from unilateral free trade does not, of course, imply that it actually gained from such a policy. McCloskey (1980) has argued that free trade harmed Britain through worsened terms of trade—i.e., that an optimal tariff was necessary. However, McCloskey's analysis was entirely based on intuition, whereas Irwin (1987) has estimated British foreign trade elasticities for that period and calculated the welfare

• Many felt that reciprocity was not an effective instrument for securing tariff reductions abroad because they felt that Britain lacked the necessary economic power. Alfred Marshall suggested that England was "not in a strong position for reprisals against hostile tariffs, because there are no important exports of hers, which other countries need so urgently as to be willing to take them from her at considerably increased cost; and because none of her rivals would permanently suffer serious injury through the partial exclusion of any products of theirs with which England can afford to dispense" (quoted in Keynes 1926, p. 408).

• In addition, some feared that Britain was more vulnerable to retaliation than other countries. In 1881 William Gladstone asked, in the *Times*,

*Can you strike the foreigners hard by retaliatory tariffs? What manufactures do you import from abroad? In all £45 million. What manufactures do you export? Nearer £200 million. . . . If you are to make the foreigner feel, you must make him feel by striking him in his largest industrial interests; but the interests which he has in sending manufactures to you is one of his smallest interests, and you are invited to inflict wounds upon yourself in the field measured by £45 million, while he has got exactly the same power of inflicting wounds upon you on a field measured by more than £200 million.*

• Marshall even suggested that infant-industry protection justified some of the foreign tariffs of Britain's new rivals, so

loss of unilateral tariff reduction at about 0.5 percent of national income in the very short run. As Irwin points out, though, longer-run elasticities imply an extremely small welfare loss, and if foreign tariff reductions are factored in (resulting from Britain's demonstration effect promoting free trade) Irwin finds that Britain was made better off. In terms of optimal policy, Irwin suggests, Britain may have timed things well by imposing trade restrictions in the 1820s and 1830s, when her monopoly power in trade was strong, and instituting gradual trade liberalization in the 1840s and thereafter as her hold on world markets was eroding.

that reciprocity was inappropriate. He wrote that "it would have been foolish for nations with immature industries to adopt England's [free trade] system pure and simple" (Keynes 1926, p. 392).

• Several economists of the time were convinced that, however sound the rationale underlying the use of tariffs for reciprocity, the policy would wind up being captured by protectionists and political interests. Marshall, after observing the American experience with protection (which reinforced his skepticism toward rational tariff intervention), felt that "in becoming intricate [protection] became corrupt, and tended to corrupt general politics" (Keynes 1926, p. 394). Marshall was not alone in this view. A 1903 manifesto signed by a number of distinguished British economists (including Francis Edgeworth, Arthur Bowley, and Edwin Cannan) and published in the *Times* warned that "protection brings in its train, the loss of purity in politics, the unfair advantage given to those who wield the powers of jobbery and corruption, unjust distribution of wealth, and the growth of sinister interests." This was undoubtedly an early manifestation of the recent developments in the theory of political economy and international trade that replaced the orthodox view that governments are benign and omnipotent with the view that their policies may reflect lobbying by pressure groups (which lobbying may lead to defects in the visible hand that outweigh ones in the invisible hand for which remedy is sought).

These arguments proved compelling at the time in Britain. But unilateralism in free trade has found little echo in other periods, including that of postwar trade liberalization. For the intellectual mainsprings for symmetric or mutual free trade (and trade liberalization), one must turn to other arguments (which I shall develop shortly).

## Postwar Theoretical Developments

It should be noted immediately that the intellectual case for free trade as a policy for maximizing national advantage, as explained above, benefited greatly from the postwar developments in the theory of commercial policy that showed that the traditional case for protection for *domestic* market failure (such as that involved in the case of infant-industry protection) was weaker than had been thought. An appropriate tariff could improve welfare over free trade; however, a more appropriate policy intervention was a domestic one, targeted directly at the source of the market failure. In jargon: The first-best policy intervention in the case of domestic distortions (or market failure) was domestic; the tariff would be a second-best policy. Tariffs were appropriate only when there was a foreign distortion (or market failure); they were the first-best policy only when there was monopoly power in external markets. Tariffs were thus demoted to a more limited role than in earlier theorizing.[16]

But even this monopoly-power-in-trade argument was called into question. It required the presence of nonnegligible market power in international markets; surely its application was limited to cases (such as jute and oil) where market shares were significant and entry was difficult. More serious, the use of tariffs to exploit monopoly power opened up the distinct possibility of retaliation—a possibility that had only been underscored by the interwar experience and the apparent reaction to the Smoot-Hawley tariff. Early theorists conjectured that though a country might reap a short-run advantage by using a tariff to exploit its market power, retali-

16. The postwar developments in the theory of commercial policy have been the work of many theorists (including Harry Johnson, T. N. Srinivasan, and Max Corden), but they originated independently with Bhagwati and Ramaswami (1963) and Meade (1951). For a statement of the theory, see Johnson 1965; for a synthesis and a generalization, consult Bhagwati 1971.

ation would leave all countries worse off. Later analysis, however, showed that an ultimate net gain, despite retaliation, could indeed be possible.[17] Although retaliation could not be demonstrated to rule out a final gain to a country adopting a tariff to exploit its monopoly power in trade, that it could immiserize such a country (and others) was analytically established, calling in doubt the wisdom of even this time-honored exception to the argument that a free trade policy would maximize a nation's welfare.

## Free Trade for One versus Free Trade for All

Because the economic theory of free trade was focused on free trade for one country rather than on free trade for all, it offers no direct guidance for the design of an international trading system or regime. Are there any indications in this body of economic thought as to what rules might be sought for the governing of trade among nations? This is certainly the kind of question that confronted the framers of GATT.

Now, there is indeed a *cosmopolitan* (as opposed to the nationalist) version of the theory of free trade. If one applies the logic of efficiency to the allocation of activity among all trading nations, and not merely within one's own nation-state, it is easy enough to see that it yields the prescription of free trade everywhere—that alone would ensure that goods and services would be produced where it could be done most cheaply. The notion that prices reflect true social costs is crucial to this conclusion, just as it is to the case for free trade for one nation alone. If any nation uses tariffs or subsidies

17. Scitovsky (1941) conjectured the immiserization of all. Using a Cournot-Nash tariff-retaliation model, Johnson (1953) demonstrated the possibility of a final net gain nonetheless. Rodriguez (1974) showed that the Johnson analysis, with quotas substituting for tariffs, would restore Scitovsky's conjecture. For an excellent review of this literature, see McMillan 1986.

(protection or promotion) to drive a wedge between market prices and social costs rather than to close a gap arising from market failure, then surely that is not consonant with an efficient world allocation of activity. The rule then emerges that free trade must apply to all.

Therefore, where the nationalist theory of free trade glosses over the use of tariffs, quotas, and subsidies by other countries, urging free trade for a nation regardless of what others do, the cosmopolitan theory requires adherence to free trade everywhere. The trade regime that one constructs must then rule out artificial comparative advantage arising from interventions such as subsidies and protection. It must equally frown upon dumping, insofar as it is a technique used successfully to secure an otherwise untenable foothold in world markets.

The two theories of free trade therefore stand in somewhat striking contrast to one another in terms of what they imply about unilateral and universal free trade.

*Darwinism and "Fairness"*

The unilateralist prescription runs into the further problem that it is at variance with the intuitive, Darwinian rationale for free trade. Think of the issue not in terms of other countries' using protection while one's own country maintains free trade (the question that nineteenth-century Britain debated, which is of equal concern to the United States today), but in terms of other countries' using export subsidies while one's own country keeps its markets open. Now, it is hard enough to cope with the demise of an industry in pursuit of the gains from trade if another country has a market-determined advantage. But if the foreign industry is backed by artificial support from its government, that often raises angry questions of "fairness."

An economist is right to claim that, if foreign governments subsidize their exports, this is simply marvelous for his own country, which then gets cheaper goods and thus should unilaterally maintain a policy of free trade. He must, however, recognize that the acceptance of this position will fuel demands for protection and imperil the possibility of maintaining the legitimacy, and hence the continuation, of free trade. A free trade regime that does not rein in or seek to regulate artificial subventions will likely help trigger its own demise. An analogy that I used to illustrate this "systemic" implication of the unilateralist position in conversing with Milton Friedman on his celebrated *Free to Choose* television series is perhaps apt: Would one be wise to receive stolen property simply because it is cheaper, or would one rather vote to prohibit such transactions because of their systemic consequences?

This line of thought supports the cosmopolitan economist's position that the world trading order ought to reflect the essence of the principle of free trade for all—for example, by permitting the appropriate use of countervailing duties and anti-dumping actions to maintain fair, competitive trade.

## GATT and Reciprocity

Indeed, that is precisely the conception that underlies GATT. Influenced by these theoretical economic considerations and by the practical political constraints on the shape of an international trade regime, GATT amounts to what I like to call a *contractarian* institution. Its underlying essence is a concept of symmetric rights and obligations for member states, rather than unilateralism in free trade.

In this sense GATT also—broadly—reflects the notion of *full* reciprocity (i.e., a broad balance of market-access obligations by the contracting parties).[18] However (in keeping with the century-old practice of most nations in reciprocal bargaining with tariff reduction, as embodied in the 1934 RTAA legislation and subsequent practice of the United States), it also incorporates the related but distinct principle of what I have called *first-difference reciprocity*—that is, tariff cuts are to proceed via bargaining that reflects a balance of perceived advantages at the margin rather than via negotiations that result in a perceived full equality of market access and reverse market access (or what, in modern American parlance, is pithily described as a "level playing field").

But this contrast between GATT's broadly contractarian, full-reciprocity goals and conception and its procedural practice of first-difference reciprocity in negotiations has built into it the possibility of tension if any major contracting party wishes to rewrite the history of accession by members to GATT and reopen the question of balance in overall market

---

18. The emphasis on reciprocity of obligations was also reinforced by the interwar experience with unilateral, self-serving but mutually destructive tariff-making and competitive exchange-rate depreciations. Nowhere is this notion better conveyed than in Robinson 1947:

*The popular view that free trade is all very well so long as all nations are free-traders, but that when other nations erect tariffs we must erect tariffs too, is countered by the argument that it would be just as sensible to drop rocks into our harbors because other nations have rocky coasts. This argument, once more, is unexceptionable on its own ground. The tariffs of foreign nations (except in so far as they can be modified by bargaining) are simply a fact of nature from the point of view of the home authorities, and the maximum of specialization that is possible in face of them still yields the maximum of efficiency. But when the game of beggar-my-neighbor has been played for one or two rounds, and foreign nations have stimulated their exports and cut down their imports by every device in their power, the burden of unemployment upon any country which refuses to join in the game will become intolerable and the demand for some form of retaliation irresistible. The popular view that tariffs must be answered by tariffs has therefore much practical force, though the question still remains open from which suit in any given circumstances it is wisest to play a card. (p. 192)*

---

access.[19] The U.S. Congress has recently been pressing for precisely this and even more,[20] with unavoidable and unfortunate consequences favorable to the politics of protection.

## Interests

Let us return to the theme of the interests that also shaped the postwar liberalization. Here, the interests as they obtained in the United States are evidently of central importance. These interests unambiguously reinforced the ideas favoring freer trade.

Structuralist political scientists have argued that dominant nations seek access to world markets, seeing in liberal trade policies and regimes their own national interest. (See Krasner 1976 and Keohane 1980.) This argument has been prompted by the fact that trade liberalization, albeit of different varieties, followed both nineteenth-century Britain's and twentieth-century America's rise to economic power. But national power in itself does not lead to liberal trade regimes; the USSR's hegemony led only to exploitation of its satellites, substituting what economists call "unrequited transfers" for "gains from trade" (Ruggie 1982). The structuralist argument requires, therefore, an added element: that the hegemonic power be capitalist.

But if the national interest of a powerful capitalist economy leads to a liberal trading regime, this national interest shades into domestic interests as constituted by the "animal spirits" of capitalists seeking outward reach, aspiring to ex-

19. The terms of accession by contracting parties to GATT are, in principle, supposed to equalize broadly the balance of overall access, in my judgment.
20. E.g., balance of mutual access is sought even at intra-sectoral levels.

ploit other countries' markets. Further, a country's ability to defy sectional interests and open its markets is likely to be enhanced by the country's rise to economic power. Power reflects prosperity, and prosperity makes the embrace of anti-protectionism easier. Indeed, there is systematic evidence (see chapter 3) to support the hypothesis that bad macroeconomics goes with bad news for freer trade: the protectionist pressures increase significantly with economic distress.

But there is a subtler issue here, reflecting back on the perception of national interest. It is one of psychology, rooted in the Darwinian conception of free trade that I sketched above. It is often argued that, in politics, free trade comes as one's ideological and policy preference only when one is strong. The Darwinian doctrine appeals to those who expect to emerge as winners, so it is preferred by nations that possess actual or perceived competitiveness. There is undoubtedly an element of truth in this, as witnessed by the reluctance of many latecomers to forgo the use of protection for their industrialization in the nineteenth and twentieth centuries. It is plausible, therefore, that the United States' embrace of postwar trade liberalization, even if actuated by the aforementioned considerations of sectional interests and national interest, was reinforced by the essential confidence in the country's likelihood of surviving—and, hence, its national interest in—the Darwinian struggle that freer trade entails.[21]

But the United States' interest in liberal trade appears to have gone beyond all this. Indeed, the executive branch of the U.S. government came to believe that the country's security interests were best served by the pursuit of liberal trade

21. The role of this Darwinian factor in the nineteenth-century experience with (unilateral) British trade liberalization, the U.S.-led postwar trade liberalization, and the current debate on U.S. trade policy is explored further in Bhagwati and Irwin 1987.

policies. On this view (most forcefully argued in recent years by the political scientist Douglas Nelson [1987]), the United States' embrace of trade liberalization was motivated not by cerebral faith in the economic virtues of free trade but by expectations that the domestic political costs of liberalization would be offset by security gains in the realm of foreign policy. Citing the triumph in the Truman Administration of the "Cold War realists," such as George Kennan, whose strategic vision emphasized the use of economic instruments to contain the Communist threat, Nelson argues[22] that

*The instruments of international economic policy (including trade policy) were seen as fundamental instruments of national security policy. The first task to which these instruments were turned was the reconstruction of a Europe seen as poised on the brink of economic collapse, with local Moscow-oriented communist parties waiting in the wings. The Marshall Plan transferred needed financial resources directly, and liberalization of the U.S. trade regime (with broad exemptions for Europe) was expected to transfer resources indirectly. (1987, p. 15)*

The belief that other nations' gains from trade would promote American security is not inconsistent with the ideological position that trade is beneficial. But this particular thesis implied a belief in the related liberal proposition that "all good things go together"[23] and reinforced in a major (per-

22. Nelson goes so far as to deny, implausibly, that direct economic gains from trade liberalization were of any consequence in U.S. policymaking, arguing that in fact these policy makers thought of trade liberalization as involving economic costs to the U.S.: "The major policy-makers in the Truman White House and State Department (Secretaries of State Marshall and Acheson in particular) not only did not perceive trade as economically advantageous but, to the extent that they considered its economic effects at all, tended to see it primarily in terms of costs." (1987, note 16)

23. See Packenham (1973) on this strand in U.S. liberal thinking in the postwar period. It is manifest in frequent assertions that population control is good not merely in itself but because it will promote peace, and that

haps decisive) way the United States' postwar commitment to a liberal trading order.

## Institutions

This commitment explains the United States' support for the General Agreement on Tariffs and Trade—which, notwithstanding all its warts, was the institution that oversaw and sustained the postwar liberalization.

Although GATT was a contractarian arrangement, the United States looked the other way when it came to requiring GATT members to fulfill symmetric obligations. In the political interest of building a stronger Europe, for example, the United States allowed asymmetrical access to markets during the long period when Europe was shifting to convertibility in current-account transactions. And the United States acquiesced in the enactment of Part IV and the granting of other special and differential treatment to developing countries, which gave them a handicap and hence an exemption from the symmetric GATT obligations which their underdeveloped status seemed to justify, much along the lines of "affirmative action" in domestic programs.

One can view the postwar period from either of two stylized perspectives. Either one can argue, with Kindleberger (1981), that the United States played a leadership role in supplying the "public good" of a GATT regime oriented toward freer trade while letting "free riders" (such as Europe in the early years of GATT, and the developing countries) escape the burden of accepting symmetric market-access obligations, or one can draw the inference that the United States

foreign aid will create prosperity and thus arrest the spread of Communism. These claims are not just ways of "selling" programs; they often reflect genuine convictions.

was acting as the leader in the sense of sustaining GATT by permitting justifiable asymmetries of obligations for these nations on a temporary basis. The latter interpretation seems more consonant with the events. It also suggests that, as these temporary circumstances ended, with the recovery of Europe and the dramatic growth of the more advanced of the newly industrialized countries, the United States would return to its original contractarian conception of GATT and begin to look for reciprocity of market access (as indeed it does today).

GATT provided the mechanism and the momentum that the ideology and the interests favoring freer trade needed in order to influence policy. Institutions create opportunities for interests, even spawning them; in turn, they are shaped by them. GATT, with its commitment to the process of freer trade and the goal of substantial free trade, provided the pro-trade forces—especially the executive branch of the U.S. government—with a vehicle for initiating and sustaining successive and successful efforts at reducing tariffs (recall figure 1). The many GATT rounds, aimed at slashing tariffs, proved effective in dealing with the ever-present protectionist pressures from constituency-conscious congressmen; they served to counter these pressures on the grounds that succumbing to them would imperil ongoing deliberations and negotiations. An ongoing, continual set of rounds was thus tactically wise as well. Washington wits have christened this the "bicycle theory": unless you keep pedaling, you will fall off.

Yet another fundamental institutional change—this one within the United States—reinforced the liberalization process and the political opposition to protection. The Smoot-Hawley fiasco had led to a transfer of tariff-setting authority from the Congress to the executive branch, which had a pro-trade bias. In itself this move imparted a powerful anti-protectionist thrust to U.S. policymaking; however, it also reinforced the pro-trade position in a subtler way. Previously, congressmen had been susceptible to direct constituency pressure, and made-to-order tariffs had emerged under Smoot-Hawley in a process of log-rolling that reflected "reciprocal noninterference" among the legislators. This stopped when the setting of individual tariffs was shifted away from the Congress. Instead, protectionist pressures now had to be concentrated on protectionist *rules*. Now narrow questions concerning the favorite tariffs of individual legislators gave way to broader questions of protectionism versus free trade. Reciprocal noninterference was replaced by lobbying, which was somewhat less unevenly divided between the protectionists and the pro-traders. For any level of protectionist pressure, the supply of protection should then fall.[24]

In the end, then, the postwar liberalization of trade can be attributed to a richly textured interplay of interests, ideology, and institutions. But during the 1970s the scene changed conspicuously. There was an onset of protection, and a widespread outbreak of protection was feared. What went wrong?

24. This argument, developed by Nelson (1987), is explored further in Hall and Nelson 1987. On other institutional matters relevant to U.S. trade policy, see Baldwin 1985b.

# The Rise of Protectionism

The downward trend in trade restrictions resulting from declining tariffs was rudely interrupted in the mid-1970s. An offsetting growth in trade barriers followed. The negotiated tariff reductions were accompanied, and their incremental effect in loosening the restraints on the world trading system was seriously compromised, by the growth of *nontariff barriers* (NTBs). Economists often refer to these barriers as *administered protection*, because they typically do not imply legislative enactment of each act of protection (although, of course, legislative consent—implicit and explicit—is necessary for the exercise of executive and quasi-judicial powers and discretion in the granting of protectionist demands made by specific petitioners and lobbies). These restrictions are customarily applied through institutions and processes set up to regulate imports, including the exercise of political power by the executive branch in making trade-restraining arrangements with other countries.

Two classes of nontariff barriers, with wholly different implications, must be distinguished: those that bypass GATT's rule of law and those that "capture" and pervert it. The former class consists of the "high-track"[1] (that is, visibly and politically negotiated) restraints on exports by trading partners; the latter class consists of "low-track" restraints, such as countervailing duties and anti-dumping provisions.

## The Growth of Nontariff Barriers

*Voluntary Export Restrictions, etc.*

The increase in high-track interventions restraining exports in one way or another has been rather dramatic since the 1970s. In 1974 the Long-Term Arrangement Regarding International Trade in Textiles became the comprehensive Multifibre Agreement, which was soon joined by steadily increasing interventions such as Orderly Marketing Agreements and Voluntary Export Restraints in industries as diverse as steel, automobiles, footwear, motorcycles, machine tools, and consumer electronics.[2]

The World Bank and the UN Conference on Trade and Development have mounted an extensive effort to calculate the incidence of nontariff barriers. The conceptual and measurement problems facing this effort are formidable. For one thing, the definition of "hard-core" NTBs that is used goes beyond voluntary export restrictions and other export-restraining arrangements to include import quotas, nonautomatic licensing, and variable levies[3]; for another, the measure

1. The distinction between the "high-track" and "low-track" processes of administered protection is drawn in Finger et al. 1982. The terminology itself is attributed to Richard Cooper.

2. The incidence of formal, negotiated restraints on manufactures during the period 1984–1986 is illustrated in figure 8.1 of the 1987 *World Development Report*.

3. Evidently, VERs are much more important in the industrialized countries, whereas import quotas and nonautomatic licensing are of

of the presence of such NTBs reflects only the percentage of imports covered by such measures, not the protective effects of the measures.[4] The orders of magnitude are, nonetheless, suggestive: In 1981, 13 percent of the imports of industrial countries were subject to such hard-core nontariff barriers; the 1986 estimate of 16 percent is broadly comparable.[5]

If one broadens the definition of NTBs to include state monopolies, import surveillance (including automatic licensing), countervailing duties, and anti-dumping provisions, the results are more compelling. Recently there has been a significant increase in this more comprehensive index of NTB coverage for all the major Organization for Economic Cooperation and Development country groups except Japan (which already had a higher initial level of NTB coverage than the European Economic Community and the United States).[6] One must be very cautious when contemplating such data, however. For instance, the inclusion of automatic licensing and of state trading in this augmented NTB index may mislead the unwary reader into an exaggerated sense of the incidence and growth of protection, since the protective effect of automatic licensing is surely negligible and since state trading may also be of no consequence.

Let us return, however, to export-restraining arrangements. By the late 1970s, voluntary export restrictions had become both significant and significantly more prevalent

corresponding importance in the developing countries. The World Bank-UNCTAD data therefore may be a good reflection of the VER situation in the industrialized countries.

4. Thus, if a VER is so effective as to rule out imports altogether, it will simply disappear from the index at hand, since the eliminated imports will not show as imports covered by VERs. Of course, the same problem afflicts the measuring of any trade restriction.

5. See *World Development Report* 1987, p. 142. The estimates for 1986 use 1981 trade weights, so comparability is facilitated.

6. See figure 5.

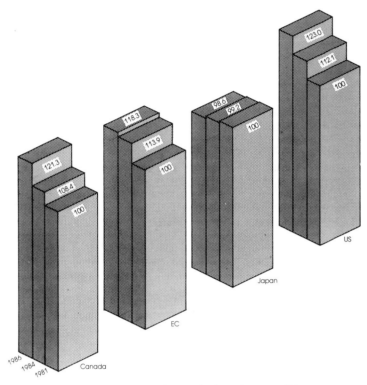

Figure 5 Import-coverage indexes of selected nontariff barriers in Canada, the European Economic Community (excluding Portugal and Spain), Japan and the United States for the years 1981–1986, where 100 is the index for 1981. (The import-coverage ratios—i.e., the sum of the value of a country's import groups affected by NTBs divided by the total value of its imports of these groups—were computed using 1981 import trade weights. Therefore, variations in the index between years can occur only if NTBs affect a different set of products or trading partners. The NTBs included are very broad in coverage, including even automatic licensing and price-control measures.) Source: UNCTAD 1987.

than GATT-approved Article XIX safeguards actions.[7] In 1982 the GATT Secretariat noted with alarm that other safeguards measures (mostly export-restraining arrangements) had been used in 63 cases since 1978, versus only 19 reported Article XIX actions.[8] The growth of this set of NTBs not only halted but partially reversed the process of trade liberalization. It also signified to many the possibility of a menacing shift in the nature of the international trade regime.

GATT represents the "rule of law." If all members play by well-defined rules—among which nondiscriminatory most-favored-nation agreements and a preference for tariffs over other trade barriers (in view of their greater transparency) are particularly important—the members must expect the chips to fall where they may. The resulting allocation of industries and trade among member countries is sacrosanct, having been legitimated by the approved process. This "fix-rule" system is in contrast to the "fix-quantity" regime that voluntary export restraints and other export-restraining arrangements (such as orderly marketing agreements) imply, for those restraints and arrangements allocate trade volumes by fiat, are often nontransparent in their protective magnitude, and necessarily lead away from most-favored-nation-based protection into discriminatory treatment of alternative suppliers.

Concern about a shift in the rules is legitimate if these developments indeed represent an enduring transition to a new fix-quantity regime. But they have their bright side: They can also be interpreted as ingenious, temporary, dam-

7. Article XIX provides for temporary protection of an industry from import competition.

8. Wolff (1983) cites this GATT study and comments that the actual ratio of VERs to Article XIX actions must have been even higher, since there was no legal need to notify the GATT of such non-GATT "extralegal" measures in the first place. For another discussion of VERs relative to Article XIX, see Hindley 1987.

age-minimizing ways in which pro-trade administrations have coped with protectionist pressures (a theme I will develop below).

---

*Countervailing Duties and Anti-Dumping Provisions: Capturing the "Fair Trade" Provisions*

An altogether different phenomenon is the translation of protectionist pressure into a "capture" of the mechanisms for maintaining fair trade—especially countervailing duties (CVDs) and anti-dumping (AD) provisions. These institutions have legitimate roles in a free trade regime, as I argued earlier, but not if they are captured and misused as protectionist instruments.

The incidence of CVD and AD actions accelerated significantly in the late 1970s. Between 1980 and 1985, "seven countries and the European Community . . . initiated 1,155 anti-dumping cases[;] there were also 425 anti-subsidy cases" (Finger and Nogues 1987, page 707). The data for CVD and AD actions by the United States, Australia, Canada, and the European Economic Community (table 2) show a preponderant reliance by the EEC on AD actions, whereas the United States was almost alone in resorting to CVDs.

The dramatic rise of such unfair-trade cases is itself *prima facie* evidence of their use for harassment of successful foreign suppliers. But the evidence in support of the capture theory is more compelling than that.

The traditional design and functioning of the national laws and institutions for initiating and settling AD and CVD complaints have encouraged the capture of these measures. For one thing, the absence of penalties for frivolous complaints means that a plaintiff often incurs only small costs, whereas a defendant (who has much to lose) often must hire the most expensive lawyers. Furthermore, although foreign firms are entitled to fair hearings, there is something to be

---

## Table 2

Countervailing duties and anti-dumping actions initiated.
(Adapted from Finger and Nogues 1987, p. 708.)

|  | United States | Australia | Canada | EEC |
|---|---|---|---|---|
| *Countervailing duties* | | | | |
| 1980 | 8[a] | 0 | 3 | 0 |
| 1981 | 10[a] | 0 | 0 | 1 |
| 1982 | 123[a] | 2 | 1 | 3 |
| 1983 | 21[a] | 7 | 3 | 2 |
| 1984 | 51[a] | 6 | 2 | 1 |
| 1985 | 39[a] | 3 | 3 | 0 |
|  | 252 | 18 | 12 | 7 |
| *Anti-dumping actions* | | | | |
| 1980 | 22[b] | 62 | 25 | 25 |
| 1981 | 14[b] | 50 | 19 | 47 |
| 1982 | 61[b] | 78 | 72 | 55 |
| 1983 | 47[b] | 87 | 36 | 36 |
| 1984 | 71[b] | 56 | 31 | 49 |
| 1985 | 65[b] | 60 | 36 | 42 |
|  | 280 | 393 | 219 | 254 |

a. U.S. Trade Act, Section 701.
b. U.S. Trade Act, Section 731.

said in favor of procedures that do not make one's nationals both the plaintiffs and the judges in a climate that is protectionist and hence prejudicial to the interests of the defendants against whom unfair trading practices are alleged.[9] (That such a prejudicial atmosphere has existed in recent years is hardly in dispute.[10])

9. Finger et al. (1982, p. 454) make the altogether different criticism that these dispute-settlement mechanisms and institutions "by design . . . [weigh] domestic producers' interests more heavily than domestic users' " and have "the capacity to impose trade restrictions but not to remove them."

10. Finger and Nogues (1987, p. 721) record that "in 1980–81, twenty-six different pieces of legislation were proposed in the U.S. Congress to deal with such matters . . . , and by the end of 1985 several hundred pieces of trade legislation had been proposed" (to deal with unfair trading practices).

The capture of these procedures by protectionists is facilitated by the fact that the descriptions and characterizations of concepts such as "fair value" (used in determining and deterring dumping) are inherently vague and can therefore be interpreted restrictively and with bias against foreign suppliers. This has indeed been happening. Norall (1986), in his review of new trends in anti-dumping practice in the EEC, documents how the Commission of the European Community (whose anti-dumping regulations reproduce, in many respects, "the bland generalities of the GATT anti-dumping code") has been able to exercise considerable discretionary power, and notes that "even though these [anti-dumping] provisions are often equivocal, they are inflexibly interpreted to provide textual justification for some very harsh results" (page 98). Norall's alarming conclusion is this:

*In a word, if certain facts are present, various aspects of the technical methodology now applied by the Commission in anti-dumping cases tend to make findings of dumping at significant levels automatic and inevitable and, secondly, to make it very difficult for exporters to modify or palliate the effect of anti-dumping duties by price increases after the imposition of duties.*

*This trend initiated in the arcane technicalities of the application of the anti-dumping regulation by the technicians—with varying degrees of tacit approval from the member countries of the European Community and those responsible for the political side of trade relations with Japan—seems to be becoming an instrument of trade policy. (pp. 98–99)*

The economist Patrick Messerlin (1987) analyzed the 515 anti-dumping cases examined between 1970 and 1985 by the Commission of the European Community and reached an equally disturbing conclusion:

*First, the EC AD procedure is now far from being marginal: it involves hundreds of cases, concerns all the important trade partners of the Community and shows increasingly restrictive outcomes. Second, there is a clear tendency for this GATT-honored procedure to generate outcomes embarrassing to GATT principles: harassment, discrimination between trade partners, nontariff barriers are intrinsic to this procedure. (page 21)*

Even the asymmetries in the ways that foreign and domestic firms are treated by those charged with determining unfair trade practices have now been fairly well documented. Fred Smith of the Competitive Enterprise Institute has remarked of U.S. practice that "if the same anti-dumping laws applied to U.S. companies, every after-Christmas sale in the country would be banned."[11] Dickey (1979) also concluded that U.S. practice had become infected by unfair asymmetries that worked against foreign firms.

The determination "fair value" proceeds relentlessly, even in cases where elementary economics would suggest that it is meaningless and that the only outcome can be a political one. For example, Poland's exports of golf carts to the United States were challenged on anti-dumping grounds. Now, there is no way in which "true" or "fair" costs and prices can be meaningfully determined for centrally planned economies in the first place. And the Poles did not even play golf, so there were no domestic prices to work with: the Poles had put the cart before the course. But protectionists do not give up. A search was mounted for "comparable" countries, whose wages and other costs would be used to reconstruct Poland's true costs, with Spain finally chosen as the ideal candidate.[12]

11. Quoted by Bovard (1987).
12. See Holzman 1983. The procedure of constructing "fair value" for CPEs from prices of non-CPE producers was built into the 1974 amend-

Even minuscule subsidies have been countervailed. Aside from the fact that the margins of errors in the calculations must greatly exceed these subsidies, their distorting effects on competition must surely be outweighed by the protectionist advantage secured by the complainants who put their foreign rivals through the CVD wringer. Bovard (1987) notes that "in 1984, Italy was convicted of a 'less-than-fair-value' margin of 1.16 percent on its pads for the keys of woodwind instruments even though [the U.S. Department of] Commerce admitted that it did not compare sales of identical products in Italy and the U.S." Kenya's carnation exports were recently countervailed at an estimated "dumping margin" of 1.58 percent. Another CVD action established the grand finding that the Thai government was subsidizing rice exports by 0.75 percent.[13]

Thus, the protective capture of CVD and AD processes is clear. Findings of minuscule "dumping margins" and subsidies, and of biases in assessing the fairness of foreign firms' trading practices, are evidence of an inappropriate use of these mechanisms. But equally important is the fact that the absence of penalties for frivolous complaints makes for a large number of cases in which the petitioner is simply seeking to tie up his successful foreign rivals in expensive defensive actions in national processes which are not exactly models of impartiality and fairness. The filing of CVD and AD complaints has a protective impact thanks to the resulting increase in the uncertainty and cost of foreign trade.

In turn, it is obvious that countervailing-duty and anti-

ment to the Anti-Dumping Act of 1921. An equally bizarre case having to do with China's exports of porcelain-on-steel cookware to the U.S. is summarized in Bovard 1987.

13. See Sathirathai and Siamwalla 1987, p. 607. The CVD procedure did not allow any offsetting adjustment for Thailand's 5 percent tax on rice exports.

dumping actions can be utilized as tactical devices to soften up one's foreign rivals and propel them and their governments into negotiating voluntary restrictions on exports. The legitimate "low-track" mechanism is then deliberately misused to pave the way for the illegitimate protectionist use of the "high-track" mechanism of administered protection. This is the considered conclusion of many careful observers. Finger and Nogues (1987) conclude that in the United States the filing of an unfair-trade-practice petition has usually paved the way for a successful attempt to get the U.S. government to protect an industry: "Large cases, the facts show, almost always begin as administered protection cases and end up as negotiated 'voluntary' export restraints (VERs) (Finger, Hall, and Nelson 1982). The United States–Japan agreement on Japanese exports of automobiles was preceded by a safeguards case.[14] The network of VERs the United States had negotiated with several steel exporters has as its antecedent a series of anti-dumping and CVD petitions." (pp. 720–721) Similarly, the recent semiconductor pact between the United States and Japan followed a blitzkrieg of anti-dumping petitions against the major Japanese manufacturers.

## Displacement versus New Protectionist Pressure

The evidence of increased nontariff barriers and administered protection just as tariffs had been reduced to new lows suggests the intriguing possibility that there may be a Law of Constant Protection: If you reduce one kind of protection, another variety simply pops up elsewhere. (You then have a Displacement Effect, not evidence of any increase in protectionist pressure.)

14. "Safeguards" cases involve requests for relief from the impact of market disruption (as under Article XIX).

But this argument is implausible. As I sketched earlier, there was indeed a dramatic conjunction of factors—drawing on ideology, interests, and institutions—that had clearly driven the engine of trade liberalization. Something surely had changed to make this engine sputter, even go into reverse. Protectionist pressures had certainly increased.

I will defer my analysis of the forces that generated this increase in protectionist pressure (among them the OPEC-led macroeconomic distress and the structural changes in the world economy) until chapter 4, where I shall consider these pro-protection forces in the context of the anti-protection forces that are being generated by other changes in the world economy.

## The Efficacy of Protection

For the moment, I will simply ask: Given that protectionist pressures increased in the mid-1970s, and that they even translated into an increasing volume of nontariff barriers, how effective was all this in restraining trade? The dog did bark, but did it bite?

Trade expansion certainly slowed down considerably between 1973 and 1983. But, as figure 2 illustrates, trade continued to grow more rapidly than income through this period. Indeed, the increase in trade-to-GNP ratios that most countries had experienced up to 1973 continued thereafter through the early 1980s. Figure 6 illustrates this striking phenomenon for Canada, Japan, South Korea, the United Kingdom, and the United States, but it exists for several other countries as well. Even the developing countries' exports of manufactures grew almost twice as rapidly as their exports to one another, registering a growth rate of over 8 percent annually during the 1970s despite sluggish growth and high rates of unemployment in the industrialized countries.

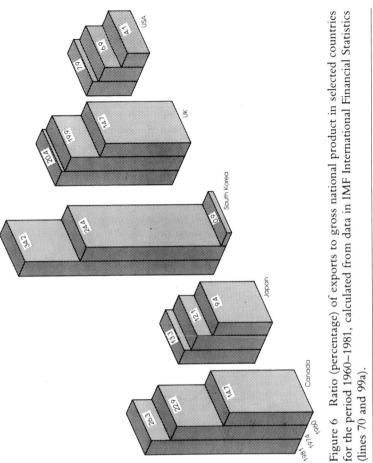

Figure 6 Ratio (percentage) of exports to gross national product in selected countries for the period 1960–1981, calculated from data in IMF International Financial Statistics (lines 70 and 99a).

Of course, world trade could have increased even more rapidly if the outbreak of nontariff barriers had been negligible.[15] In the present instance, however, it is plausible to maintain that the growth of nontariff barriers had, at worst, a moderately adverse effect on the growth of trade. Why?

This puzzle, in which the growth of protection appears significant but its consequences do not,[16] can be explained by drawing on, and adapting to our purpose, recent writings by Robert Baldwin (1982, 1985a). Baldwin reminds us that protection is often less than appearances would suggest, because there are many ways in which exporting countries can get around it and continue to increase their export earnings:

*Consider the response of exporting firms to the imposition of tighter foreign restrictions on imports of a particular product. One immediate response will be to try to ship the product in a form which is not covered by the restriction. . . . One case involves coats with removable sleeves. By importing sleeves unattached, the rest of the coat comes in as a vest, thereby qualifying for more favorable tariff treatment. . . . The use of substitute components is another common way of getting around import restrictions. The quotas on imports of sugar into the United States only apply to pure sugar, defined as 100 percent sucrose. Foreign exporters are avoiding the quotas by shipping sugar products consisting mainly of sucrose, but also containing a sugar substitute, for example, dextrose. . . . At one time, exporters of running shoes to the United States avoided the high tariff on rubber footwear by using leather for most of the upper portion of the shoes, thereby qualifying for duty treatment as leather shoes. (page 110)*

15. We economists always worry about getting our counterfactual scenarios right; without a yardstick, we are paralyzed. There is an apocryphal story about an economist who, when asked "How is your wife?," replied: "Compared to what?"

16. This puzzle was first noted by Hughes and Krueger (1984), in the context of developing countries' exports.

The ineffectiveness of trade barriers is even more apparent in the case of voluntary export restrictions and similar *export*-restraint arrangements than in the case of import tariffs. In choosing them in preference to tariffs sanctioned by Article XIX, the negotiating countries may well have opted for the least damaging way of responding to protectionist demands that could not be successfully rejected outright. I have recently argued (Bhagwati 1986, 1987) that some industries (e.g., footwear) seem to have two characteristics that lend support to this "VERs as porous protection" model as an explanation of why the trade-destroying effect of protection may have been contained:

• Undifferentiated products (such as the cheaper varieties of garments and footwear) are easy to "trans-ship"—that is, to cheat on the rules of origin by passing off products of a country restricted by VERs as products of countries not covered by VERs.

• Low start-up costs, and the attendant small recoupment horizons, facilitate the shifting of investments (and hence of products) to adjacent countries not covered by VERs, so that an exporting country can—at some cost—get around VERs by "investment-shunting" of its firms to sources unaffected by VERs.[17]

In such industries, voluntary export restraints can yield a "close to free trade" solution for the exporting countries that are afflicted by them. These countries can continue to profit from their comparative advantage by exploiting—legally (through investment-shunting) and illegally (through trans-shipment)—the fact that VERs do not apply to "third

17. This strategy allows the exporter to recover his investment costs, since it is usually some time before the VERs are extended to cover these alternative sources (or until the VERs are eliminated as the political pressure subsides, as happened in the case of U.S. footwear imports).

countries," whereas importing-country tariffs do.[18] The complaisance of the VER-afflicted exporters in regard to having VERs imposed (rather than being hit by import tariffs, as GATT Article XIX requires) is, therefore, easy enough to understand.[19]

But the question then arises: Why would the protecting importing countries prefer this "porous protection?" Does it not imply less protection than the industry would have under a corresponding import restraint? Indeed it does. But therein lies its attractiveness.

If a country's executive branch is characterized by the pro-trade bias I sketched above whereas its legislators must respond to protectionist pressure from various constituency groups, then it can be argued that a smart executive branch will prefer to use a porous form of protection that, while ensuring freer market access, will nonetheless appear to be a concession to political demands for protection from the legislators or from their constituencies. No doubt the protectionist constituencies and their legislative spokesmen will eventually complain about continuing imports; but then the executive branch will be able to cite its VER actions, promise to look into complaints and perhaps bring other countries into the VER net, and continue to obfuscate and buy time

18. Of course, the VERs in this instance represent only a partial and suboptimal approximation to the free-trade solution, which remains the desirable but infeasible alternative. Moreover, not all exporting countries are capable of the flexible and shrewd response that underlies the model of porous protection sketched above.

19. In the case of *effective* VERs, on the other hand, trade would indeed be restricted and we could not explain why trade would grow despite VERs. In these cases, however, the transfer of rents (on scarce imports) from the importing to the exporting country generally follows under VERs relative to import tariffs, and this too can provide a reason for their appeal to the exporting countries. For theoretical analyses of this rent-transfer rationale for VERs, and qualifications to it, see Brecher and Bhagwati 1987 and Dinopoulos and Kreinin 1987a.

without effectively protecting.[20] The nontransparency of VERs then is an advantage, not a hindrance, to the continuation of relatively free (although not free and undistorted) trade as long as the obfuscation does not become apparent before the industry has adjusted to the fact of effective foreign rivalry.

I do not put forth this view out of complacency about the growth of these discriminatory trade restraints. If they were to become an enduring trade regime, we would indeed have shifted to a fix-quantity system for overseeing international trade, in contradiction to all that good Economics implies. That was the apprehension of Jan Tumlir, who long guided the GATT Secretariat with distinction.[21] He feared, in fact, that the fix-quantity regime was already here. I am suggesting a more benign perspective on these practices: that they indicate the ingenuity and vigor with which governments have striven to maintain a pro-trade bias in the face of a difficult resurgence of protectionist pressures in the last decade.

This benign assessment still leaves open the question of how the institutions should be changed to prevent these practices from acquiring long-term legitimacy and undermining the fix-rule trading system. I shall turn to this in a later chapter, after examining the changes in the world economy that, through their effects on interests, bear on the question of protectionism.

20. This "two-headed" version of governments underlies the Feenstra-Bhagwati (1982) model of the efficient tariff, which postulates that one branch of the government (pursuing special interests) interacts with a protectionist lobby to enact a political-economy tariff. Then another branch of the government—pursuing the national interest—uses the revenue generated by this tariff to bribe the lobby into accepting a less harmful tariff that nonetheless leaves it as well off as under the political-economy tariff.

21. See Tumlir 1985.

# Structural Change and Interdependence

**4**

Let me begin this chapter by considering the impact on the rise of protectionism of the macroeconomic difficulties that ensued as the world struggled with dramatically increasing oil prices in the 1970s.

As it happens, the association between high rates of unemployment, excess capacity, recessions in general, and the growth of protectionist pressures—evident to economists since the interwar years—has been confirmed by econometric analysis. Tackacs (1981) analyzed time-series data on the number of safeguards petitions filed by industries seeking import relief in the United States between 1949 and 1979 and found that the pressure for protection, so measured, does indeed increase with adverse macroeconomic conditions. Fewer safeguards cases were initiated the higher the real gross national product, the lower the unemployment rate, and the higher the rate of capacity utilization (Tackacs 1981, p. 689).[1]

---

1. Cassing et al. (1986) have proposed an interesting theory as to how differences in regional interests in the U.S. can produce a tariff cycle by intensifying protectionist pressures at a cyclical trough. Their argument depends on the greater political weight in the U.S. of the old import-competing regions than of the old export-oriented regions. This creates the following dynamics: "When general economic conditions are poor, the old import-competing regions will join the protectionist coalition, and pres-

## Structural Change

The protectionist forces unleashed by the macroeconomic distress of the late 1970s and the recession of the early 1980s were, however, reinforced by structural changes in the world economy.

Among these changes were the emergence of Japan and the newly industrialized countries (NICs) as important competitors in manufactures on the international scene and the decline of the United States in relation to world income and trade. The former created new problems of adjustment for specific industries, and even a general fear of deindustrialization and its mythical, metaphysical, monstrous consequences for one's well-being. The latter change created a psychological trauma in the United States. The resulting "diminished giant" syndrome made it hard for many Americans to accept the successes of the emergent trading nations, and there was a tendency to attribute those successes to unfair trading practices and underhanded, extralegal tactics. The suspicions seemed to justify retaliatory protection, and they brought demands for fix-quantity outcomes from one's trading rivals.

### The Double Squeeze

The growth of exports from Japan and the Pacific "Gang of Four" (Singapore, Hong Kong, South Korea, and Taiwan),[2]

sures for tariffs will increase. Although export-oriented old regions will be joining a free-trade coalition at the same time, in a political system where old import-competing regions outweigh old exporting regions, the activation of the old regions on both sides will favor the protectionists. Conversely, during cyclical peaks, when both types of old regions desert their respective coalitions, the protectionist coalition will suffer a relatively greater loss in political strength. It is thus at the peaks that the free traders have their best winning chances." (p. 860)

2. The popular epithet Gang of Four seemed apt when I came up with it in jest, since the extraordinary performance of these Pacific nations put them

and the less spectacular but still impressive export performance of other NICs (such as Brazil) and of Newly Exporting Countries (such as Malaysia and Thailand), has created
problems for *specific* industries in the OECD countries, neces-
sitating that they adjust to these changes. (See Hughes and
Newberry 1986 for a detailed analysis of the export performance of NECs.)

A country that grows more rapidly than others will, on
average, export at a volume and a growth rate that are hard
for the other countries to accommodate without complaints
from the domestic industries that must bear the brunt of the
adjustment. Japan has been up against this phenomenon since
the 1930s. Even then, when Japan was not yet dominant,
Japanese diplomats were scurrying around negotiating voluntary export restraints on pencils, electric lamps, safety
matches, and other products with the United States, the
United Kingdom, Australia, and other trading partners—
partners among whom a bilateral surplus in trade with Japan
was common. The present surplus situation has compounded
Japan's difficulties; however, even if her surplus were to disappear, Japan would continue to attract the protectionist ire
of disaffected competitors (see Bhagwati 1986b).

This problem of adjustment has been compounded by
the simultaneous expansion of exports from the NICs and
NECs. The double squeeze, however, constitutes double
jeopardy for the pro-trade protagonists. Not only does it
augment the pressure on specific industries to adjust, but it
also tends to create a bimodal pressure at both ends of the
manufacturing spectrum. While the old labor-intensive industries are in combat with the NECs and the NICs, the new
high-tech industries are up against Japan and the more ad-

in a separate class among the developing countries. These countries are also
known as the Four Tigers.

---

vanced NICs as well. With both sunset and sunrise industries therefore in apparent peril, the fear has grown, especially in the United States and the United Kingdom, that only the scorching sun will survive for their benefit, with arid "deindustrialization" their destiny!

Thus, in 1982 Walter Mondale complained: "We've been running up the white flag when we should be running up the American flag. . . . What do we want our kids to do? Sweep up around the Japanese computers?"[3] During his unsuccessful presidential campaign of 1984, Mondale invoked images of Americans reduced to flipping hamburgers at McDonalds while the Japanese overwhelmed the country's industries. He might have invoked, with greater irony, a picture of American kids rolling rice cakes at sushi bars.

The fear of deindustrialization has also agitated the leaders of trade unions in declining, protection-seeking industries. Sol Chaikin of the International Garment Workers' Union has protested. "Because there are relatively few well-paying jobs in the service sector, an economy devoid of manufacturing would also necessarily experience a general decline in living standards. . . . Unrestricted trade and the investment practices of the multinationals . . . can only lead to an America ultimately devoid of manufacturing." (1982, p. 848) But his lament pales beside the late Theodore White's exclamation that "the Japanese are on the move again in one of history's most brilliant commercial offensives, as they go about dismantling American industry" (1985, p. 23).

The agitation of specific industries under pressure defines the accentuation of protectionist sectional interests; the fear of deindustrialization compounds it with the protectionist redefinition of "national interest." (The latter phenomenon is widespread and important; the dubious economics of

3. *New York Times*, October 13, 1982, p. A3.

the deindustrialization complex will therefore be examined in chapter 5.)

---

## The "Diminished Giant" Syndrome

For the United States, the problem has been complicated further by the relative decline in the national economy. While it continues to be a dominant power, the United States has witnessed the erosion of its predominant status in the world economy as Japan has risen from the ashes and as other Pacific nations have emerged onto the scene.

The parallel with Britain at the end of the nineteenth century is dramatic. In both instances, the giant's diminution produced a protectionist backlash, sorely trying the pro-trade bias of the international regime.[4] Walter Lippmann characterized this as the American Century. In the same vein, the nineteenth century was Britain's. As the century ended, Britain was gradually losing her political and economic preeminence. The twentieth century is ending similarly for the United States. Linder (1986) has already announced the arrival of the Pacific Century.

The end of the Napoleonic wars and the coming of the Industrial Revolution saw Britain emerge as the unchallenged leader among nations. The end of the Second World War, with the destruction of industrial capacity in Europe and Japan, saw the United States attain a similar position. However, neither country could seriously hope to maintain its status once other countries industrialized or regained their industrial potential. (One difference, of course, is that the United States encouraged and promoted economic recovery in Europe and Japan in the early postwar period, whereas Britain did not actively court the industrialization of Continental Europe and the United States.)

---

4. Here I again draw extensively on Bhagwati and Irwin 1987.

---

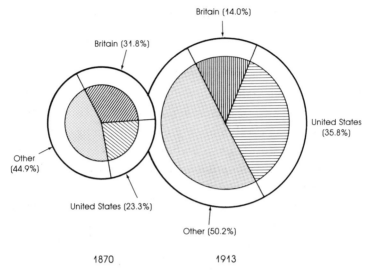

Britain (14.0%)

Britain (31.8%)

United States
(35.8%)

Other
(44.9%)

United States (23.3%)

Other (50.2%)

1870

1913

Figure 7    Shares of Britain and the United States in world industrial
production, 1870 and 1913. Source: Crouzet 1982.

The inevitable relative declines of Britain and the United
States were manifested in decreases in the sizes of their economies in relation to the world economy.

From 1870 to 1913, Britain's share of world industrial
production fell from 31.8 percent to 14.0 percent. Over the
same period, Germany's share rose somewhat and the United
States expanded its share from 23.3 percent to 35.8 percent
(figure 7). Similarly, the United States has seen its share of
world output decline since the Second World War. In 1950
the United States accounted for 40.3 percent of total world
gross domestic product; by 1980 the figure was down to 21.8
percent. Over the same period, Europe's share of the world
GDP increased from 21.2 percent to 29.8 percent and Japan's
from 1.6 percent to 8.8 percent (figure 8). The developing
countries boosted their share from 12.7 percent to 17.9 percent over the same period. (UNCTAD 1983, pp. 446–447)

Both countries saw their shares of world trade decline as

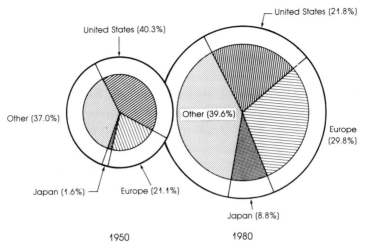

Figure 8    Shares of the United States, Europe, and Japan in world gross domestic product, 1950 and 1980. Source: UNCTAD 1983.

well. From 1880 to 1913, Britain's share of world manufactured exports fell from 41.1 percent to 29.9 percent. Over the same period, the United States expanded its share from 7.8 percent to 12.6 percent and Germany increased its share from 19.3 percent to 26.5 percent. (Saul 1965, p. 12) In 1950, U.S. exports accounted for 16.7 percent of the value of total world exports; by 1980 this share was 10.9 percent. During this period, Europe's share increased from 33.4 percent to 40.4 percent and Japan's from 1.4 percent to 6.4 percent. (UNCTAD 1983, pp. 2, 3, 35)

The diminution in Britain's preeminence in the world economy led to a rise in protectionist sentiments and to demands for an end to Britain's unilateralist embrace of free-trade principles, and the United States has similarly been witnessing protectionist pressures. The present-day movement is aimed pointedly at the newly successful rivals, just as its predecessor was. The United States and Germany were to

Britain what the Pacific nations—Japan in particular—are to the United States today.[5]

During the 1870s and the 1880s, Britain witnessed the rise of the National Fair Trade League, the National Society for the Defense of British Industry, and the Reciprocity Fair Trade Association. Today the United States witnesses demands for full reciprocity, for "level playing fields," and for "fair trade," all of them predicated on a self-serving "I am more open than thou" presumption against the new economically successful rivals.

Whereas the British fair-traders were trying to reverse a long-standing commitment to unilateral free trade, and fueling protectionist pressures in consequence, the American fair-traders have directed their efforts at a pro-trade executive branch that certainly is not unilateralist in ideology or in policy. The contention that "foreign markets are closed while ours are open" reflected policy and reality in the British episode. It does not for the United States today, where the advocacy of fair trade is more reflective of the psychological mood of a nation losing hegemony in the world economy. This creates the perception that, if markets are getting tighter and Japan is more successful in penetrating them, this is *ipso facto* evidence of inscrutable and asymmetric Japanese barriers to trade.

In truth, Japan's tariffs are among the lowest in the world. However, much anecdotal evidence has been cited in support of the claim that somehow, in an obscure but effective fashion, Japan has been significantly protecting her manufactures and importing less than she should—and indeed, like other nations, Japan does some foolish things that, given the intense scrutiny she has received, it is unwise to be

5. The British reciprocitarians took aim at the "deliberate and deadly rivalry" provoked by Germany and the United States, matching the recent Japanophobic sentiments on trade. See Bhagwati and Irwin 1987, p. 119.

'The new British lightweight Walkman for instance! Why won't you people buy it?'

This Mac cartoon from London's *Daily Mail* ridicules the often exaggerated and unfair allegations by protectionists against foreign rivals' unfair trading practices.

doing. For example, I have been told that the Dutch export tulip bulbs to almost every country except Japan because the Japanese insist on checking them by cutting the stems vertically down the middle, and even Japanese ingenuity cannot put them back together again. But we economists are trained not to go by anecdotal evidence. Aside from the fact that such evidence may be self-serving when the source is an interested exporter, it may simply be misleading, because inference of significant incidence and protectionist impact from anecdotes may be unwarranted.

It is important, therefore, to note that recent econometric studies are divided on the issue of Japanese protectionism. The early work of Saxonhouse (1983) and the sophisticated recent analysis of Noland (1987) conclude strongly that Japan cannot plausibly be said to be importing less than what cross-country evidence would lead us to expect her to import; Balassa (1986) modifies Saxonhouse's regressions to argue that Japan's imports-to-GNP ratio is low, and Lawrence (1987) (who looks only at intra-industry trade) also finds Japan's imports to be low. Most professional opinion, however, remains skeptical of claims that Japan is unfairly and asymmetrically denying access to its markets in manufactures. Even if Japan's imports are "low," this may be due to cultural factors rather than to underhanded and illegitimate trade practices. Nonetheless, the suspicion lingers; indeed, the belief in Japan's perfidy is often unshakable.

Thus, whereas the above-described "double squeeze" has stoked the protectionist fires directly, the "diminished giant" syndrome has done so indirectly by encouraging the notion that other countries are trading unfairly and that this calls for aggressive trade legislation, tougher and more restrictive interpretations of unfair trade practices, "hardball" international negotiations, and confrontational tactics. This is evident from the trade legislation pending in the U.S. Congress today; it also explains well the capture of the countervailing-duty and anti-dumping mechanisms by protection-seeking interests.

The "diminished giant" syndrome was accentuated by the macroeconomic difficulties, the sluggish growth, and the high unemployment rates of the 1970s. Those years also brought other events that strengthened the anti-trade forces in the United States. The recycling of OPEC funds to South America, hailed at the time as a triumph of U.S. banking and as evidence of the virtues of the marketplace, left the world economy in a debt crisis. This, and the creditor-imposed deflationary bias in debtor countries, resulted in a loss of export markets in Latin America for U.S. manufactures and a deepening of the adjustment imposed on specific sectors.

The rise of the dollar, a consequence of the expansionary

fiscal and deflationary monetary policy mix in the United States and the enormous influx of foreign funds into the United States, also levied a toll. It required, in turn, a squeeze of the traded sector: export and import-competing industries had to contract relative to nontraded sectors in consequence, deepening their distress and fueling demands for protectionism. In essence, the dollar was "overvalued" in the sense that the capital account was driving the current account; the dollar was rising because of capital influx and, in turn, affecting the trade flows.

The last-mentioned problem has now become a *systemic* one (owing to the unprecedented integration of financial markets in the major OECD countries, which creates the potential for significant capital-account-driven changes in exchange rates, with consequent pressures for protection in the countries experiencing "overvaluation"). Indeed, the close integration of financial markets across countries and the sheer volume of funds accentuate the vulnerability of the international system through the consequent volatility of exchange rates, which makes protectionist demands more likely. The choice seems to lie between managed exchange rates and managed trade.

## Interdependence

The structural factors I have just sketched have surely contributed to the recent protectionist pressures. There are, however, other factors that are creating interests favorable to freer trade. They arise from the increased globalization and interdependence in the world economy, through trade and direct foreign investment. Their impact has been obscured by the protectionism of the last decade, but their emergence and their promise cannot be doubted.

## The Traditional Imbalance of Interests

International economists have long been frustrated by the dissonance between the elegance of their irrefutable demonstration of the advantages of free trade and the inelegance with which practical politics embraces protection. This incongruence did not escape the keen eye of Vilfredo Pareto. In his *Manual of Political Economy* (1927), Pareto sought to explain it within an analytical framework[6] by citing the imbalance of interests that predisposes pluralistic politics toward protection:

*Even if it were very clearly demonstrated that protection always entails the destruction of wealth, if that were taught to every citizen just as they learn the abc's, protection would lose so small a number of partisans and free trade would gain so few of them that the effect can be almost, or even completely, disregarded. The motives which lead men to act are quite different. (p. 377)*

*In order to explain how those who champion protection make themselves heard so easily, it is necessary to add a consideration which applies to social movements generally. The intensity of the work of an individual is not proportionate to the benefits which that work may bring him nor to the harm which it may enable him to avoid. If a certain measure A is the case of the loss of one franc to each of a thousand persons, and of a thousand franc gain to one individual, the latter will expend a great deal of energy, whereas the former will resist weakly; and it is likely that, in the end, the person who is attempting to secure the thousand francs via A will be successful.*

*A protectionist measure provides large benefits to a small number of people, and causes a very great number of consumers a slight loss. This circumstance makes it easier to put a protection measure into practice. (p. 379)*

---

6. Pareto's analysis foreshadows the seminal work of Mancur Olson (1965).

---

The general failure of consumers to exercise countervailing power to oppose and offset the interests of producers (whether out of ignorance or because it does not pay any one consumer to incur the cost of lobbying for a policy whose benefits will be spread thinly over many consumers) is not the only ill that afflicts the opponents of protectionism.

One would also hope to see countervailing power exercised by the export interests that would suffer from protection, for, if protection favors the import-competing industries, it simultaneously discourages other industries, among them the export industries. Indeed, there is abundant empirical evidence that protectionist regimes exhibit dismal export performance.[7] But one must make an intellectual effort to see this connection. Indeed, it is not uncommon to find trained economists who fail to grasp the relationship. It is not surprising, therefore, that export interests have not generally been mobilized in opposition to import-competing industries' demands for protection.[8]

---

*Interdependence and Changing Interests*

The enormous growth of trade and of direct foreign investment not for host-country markets but for export into home and world markets, has begun to change the situation significantly.

---

7. See the recent evidence reviewed in Bhagwati 1978 and Krueger 1978. Pareto (1927, p. 381) seems to have been quite determined on this question: ". . . one obtains a practical confirmation of the assertion that protection, in reducing imports, also decreases exports. This phenomenon has been observed in a great number of cases and for many countries."

8. However, a recent statistical analysis of the U.S. House of Representatives' vote on a bill pertaining to "domestic content" in automobiles (McArthur and Marks 1988) suggests that export interests, proxied by the percentage of each state's labor force directly involved in the constituency's production of manufactures for export, increased the probability of a negative vote on this protectionist bill. But this finding almost certainly reflects, rather, the new politics of anti-protectionism arising from global interdependence, which I discuss below.

---

As I have already remarked, most countries' trade-to-GNP ratios continued to increase even through the sluggish 1970s. For the industrialized countries together, Michaely (1977) has estimated that the import-to-GDP ratio increased from 13.0 percent to 17.0 percent (and, excluding oil, from 11.7 percent to 13.9 percent) between 1973 and 1979. The implied 2.9 percent annual rate of increase in this index of trade interdependence was almost identical to its 2.8 percent annual rate of increase during the more prosperous years between 1960 and 1973. Along with this increase in trade, export markets and interests have diversified and have become more significant.

Moreover, direct foreign investment (DFI) in the developing countries—which at one time was geared to sheltered home markets—has increasingly shifted to multinational corporations, which invest in one market in pursuit of lower costs to export to others. This has resulted in a great deal of international criss-crossing of DFI.

We are also long past the days of one-way DFI of the sort that was alarmingly portrayed in Servan-Schreiber's 1968 book *The American Challenge.* Cross-investments between countries occur with greater frequency today. These cross-investments are not merely DFI by one country in the other country in industries different from those where the latter country undertakes DFI in the former country; often there are intra-industry cross-investments such that multinational corporations in the same industry penetrate each other's home base, and occasionally they even export back to the home market and elsewhere.[9] Joint production ventures and production-cum-marketing arrangements, which are also

9. In 1987, Honda (an early investor in the U.S.) announced a 4-year plan to expand its U.S. production so as to export roughly 50,000 cars back to Japan (*New York Times*, September 18).

increasingly common, result in incestuous cross-country relationships among multinational corporations that are otherwise in competition.

In consequence, we are faced with what might be called a "spider's web" phenomenon—production is globalized through a web of criss-crossing DFIs and lesser relationships. An important aspect of this phenomenon, recently investigated in depth by Lipsey and Kravis (1986) for the United States, is revealing and has important implications for the emergence of pro-trade interests.

Lipsey and Kravis's examination of the worldwide exports of the United States, its multinational corporations, and their majority-owned affiliates abroad for the years 1966 through 1983 reveals two dramatic facts: (1) In 1966 the "offshore" exports by the foreign affiliates were already equal to more than 25 percent of the "mainland" U.S. exports, and by 1983 this ratio had increased to nearly 75 percent. (2) The U.S. parent corporations' "mainland" exports exceeded their affiliates' "offshore" exports by 1977 (figure 9). Evidently, offshore production for global markets has become a predominant reality. But then, this phenomenon has also been observed in the case of Swedish multinationals (Blomström 1986) and in the case of Switzerland (Borner 1986).[10]

This globalization creates an increasingly important, pro-trade interest and voice in the arena where protectionist forces seek to triumph. The pro-trade activity that follows is largely a matter of undertaking prudential opposition to protectionism at home to avoid a possible outbreak of protectionism elsewhere. Such an outbreak, by closing markets everywhere, would imperil the returns to global investments designed for exports to the world's markets. Hence, this interest does not oppose specific acts of sectoral protection;

10. See also Swedenborg 1982 and Borner and Wehrle 1984.

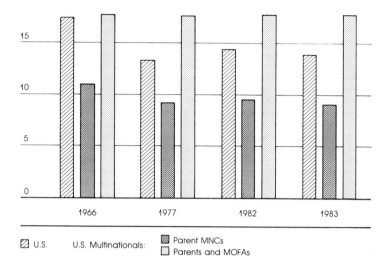

☑ U.S.     U.S. Multinationals:     ▓ Parent MNCs
                                     ▒ Parents and MOFAs

Figure 9   Percentage shares in world exports of the United States
and of U.S. multinational corporations (MNCs) and their majority-
owned foreign affiliates (MOFAs) for the years 1966–1983. Source:
Lipsey and Kravis 1986.

rather, it operates at a high level, mobilizing opinion and
lobbying against protectionism more generally. We thus
witness the chief executive officers of various multinational
corporations taking the high road on deploring protection;
and we also find them supportive of liberal "think tanks" and
of institutions (such as the Trilateral Commission) which are
primarily cosmopolitan and anti-protectionist in their ideological orientation and which help to make the policy ethos
favorable to the idea of keeping markets open.

To look for the pro-trade influence of multinational corporations in cases of successful opposition to particular protectionist pressures (e.g., to suggest that the Kennedy Round
or the Tokyo Round tariff reductions should be greater

where there is greater DFI in the industry or greater intra-firm international trade between parents and foreign affiliates) is, therefore, to seek evidence of multinationals' influence at too low a level. It is like looking for a ham sandwich at the Lord Mayor's banquet. It is not surprising, therefore, that the attempts of Helleiner (1977) and Lavergne (1983) to do precisely this through regression analysis of U.S. data on tariff reductions in the Kennedy and Tokyo Rounds have produced dismal results.[11]

But the "spider's web" phenomenon does occasionally translate into effective opposition to specific, sectoral protectionism. For example, in 1985, when American semiconductor firms were first getting together to initiate an antidumping action against Japanese producers of the memory microchips known as EPROMs (erasable programmable

---

11. The regression approach to explaining the variations in tariff cuts in the Kennedy Round (and other rounds) by reference to variables such as adjustment costs was pioneered by my MIT student John Cheh (1974). I had been unhappy with attempts by Beatrice Vaccara, Georgio Basevi, and others who had treated existing tariff structures as the dependent variable to be so explained. I felt that the tariff structure was an accretion of many historical influences, and a good $R^2$ on such exercises was beside the point. However, variations in tariff *cuts* in the Kennedy Round provided an excellent approximation to a controlled experiment in getting at factors that influenced tariffs. I therefore asked Cheh in 1972 to examine the Kennedy Round from this point of view. When his findings suggested that the across-the-board tariff cuts were moderated for industries with labor-adjustment costs, I also interpreted them for him in terms of the government's having a noneconomic objective of moderating short-term labor-adjustment costs, along the lines of the theory of noneconomic objectives such as self-sufficiency, restricting luxury consumption, etc. Corden (1974) has independently formulated a related, and more restrictive, noneconomic objective: that governments seek to preserve the status quo in incomes, preventing a fall in them for any group.

Lavergne's (1983) regression exercises basically build on the approach of Cheh, but in the matter of multinationals and their influence I find this attempt not meaningful (and hence his lack of results unsurprising), for reasons explained in the text.

---

read-only memories), noticeably absent were Motorola and Texas Instruments, who produced semiconductors in Japan and expected to ship them to the United States (Miller 1985). The recent attempts in the U.S. Congress to punish Toshiba for its sale of sensitive propeller-milling equipment to the Soviet Union by selectively proscribing imports of its products posed great difficulty from the outset, since it was hard to exclude imports of most Toshiba products without hurting articulate domestic consumers, producers, and dealers.[12]

Furthermore, trade and direct foreign investment may drive a sector of a country's economy that is a potential target of protectionism into the anti-protection camp through the creation of "hostages." In this game, a country whose export in a given sector is threatened with barriers threatens retaliatory barriers against a potentially articulate and effective exporter in the offending country.[13] A classic instance of this is China's successful resistance to harshly restrictive quotas in the last Multifibre negotiations. China's threat to reduce

12. Even then, the final choice of the products whose importation would be curtailed prompted fresh opposition from several major American high-technology corporations on the grounds that their own production would be severely handicapped by the proposed bans. (See "Top U.S. Corporations Lobbying Against Curb on Toshiba Imports," *New York Times*, September 14, 1987.) These corporations include AT&T, General Electric, Honeywell, Hewlett-Packard, IBM, Motorola, Rockwell International, and Xerox—some of the biggest in the U.S. Paul Freedenberg, the Assistant Secretary of Commerce, is quoted as saying: "We're talking about major multinationals and consumer electronics companies. There are a whole slew of household names that have a relationship with Toshiba."

13. Although increased linkage creates the possibility of more such hostage-taking, it is not always easy to find industries that are willing to be used in this strategic game. They may reap short-term windfall profits from retaliatory protection imposed on their competing imports, but they tend to react negatively because such protection, being short-term and geared only to retaliation, only disrupts settled market conditions and may invite retaliation and retribution on themselves in turn.

grain imports from the United States galvanized the export-seeking American farm lobby into action.

## DFIs and Responses to Import Competition: Increasing Alternatives

Increased trade and the *actual* globalization of the world economy through criss-crossing direct foreign investment are not the only things that create pro-trade interests. The *potentiality* of DFI is another. It undermines protectionism by providing an alternative to protection as a form of adjustment to import competition.

One frequent option for an industry faced with import competition is to shift production to the very location that gives the foreign competitor its cost advantage. This response is likely when the industry is innovative, and simply suffers from the high cost of its domestic location; it is less likely in the case of a senescent, technically stagnant, labor-intensive industry (Bhagwati 1982a, 1986a). Since, however, this is the capitalist response, rather than that of industry-specific labor unions (to which it poses the threat of job losses), the option of undertaking DFI abroad tends to weaken the occasional alliance between these two pressure groups for protectionist lobbying (see Magee 1980).

But organized labor also seems at times to have caught on to this game; it is not averse to using threats of protection to induce DFI from foreign competitors. (For example, the United Auto Workers appear to have helped induce Japanese investments in the American auto industry, although that union sides with protection in domestic politics.) We have here a generic phenomenon whereby DFI is undertaken by Japanese exporting firms to "buy off" the local pressure groups of firms and/or unions who otherwise threaten continued legislative pressures for tariffs to close the import markets. In the 1980s this type of protectionist-threat-induced, "*quid pro quo*" investment in the United States by Japanese firms appeared to be a growing phenomenon.[14] It represented yet another alternative to old-fashioned tariff-making.

## Harnessing Export Interests

Thus, both the reality and the potential of increased trade and foreign investment linkages in the world economy are significant new sources of pro-trade and anti-protection politics.

Another element in the picture has been the embrace and cultivation of export interests by the Reagan administration. This strategy is aimed at countervailing and containing political pressure for protection by encouraging pro-trade interests. But it is also expected to work by deflecting the political agenda from "closing your markets" (i.e., protectionist outcomes) to "opening their markets" (i.e., pro-trade outcomes). This is another case of the ingenuity and quick-footedness of a pro-trade executive branch in coping with the rise of protectionist pressures. But this silver cloud has a black lining: Care will have to be exercised to ensure that the opening-of-markets tactic does not undermine the tenets of GATT's fix-rule, most-favored-nation-centered regime. Let me explain.

14. The term "*quid pro quo* DFI" was introduced in Bhagwati 1985b and Bhagwati 1986a. Japan's Ministry of International Trade and Industry recently completed a survey of Japanese DFI abroad and found that a large fraction of the respondents cited reasons of the *quid pro quo* variety to explain their investment decisions. (I am indebted to Professor Shishido of the International University of Japan for this information.) The subsequent dramatic shift in the yen-dollar exchange rate has made such *quid pro quo* DFI pay off substantial dividends and ushered back into the picture more conventional reasons for Japanese firms to invest in the U.S.

See the theoretical modeling of *quid pro quo* DFI in Bhagwati, Brecher, Dinopoulos, and Srinivasan 1987 and in Bhagwati and Dinopoulos 1986. For recent analyses, see Dinopoulos 1987 and Wong 1987.

There are two fundamental ways in which the co-opting of export interests has figured in U.S. trade policy: first, by multilateral attempts at liberalizing world trade in new sectors, where the United States—once lukewarm about and even opposed to freer trade—now perceives its comparative advantage; second, by bilateral attempts at opening markets in these sectors as well as in the traditional area of manufactures.

The *multilateral* efforts to liberalize trade have been centered primarily on services and on agriculture. The attempt by the United States to bring services into GATT negotiations, and even to incorporate services into GATT formally, began at the November 1982 GATT inter-ministerial meetings and finally succeeded at Punta del Este in the summer of 1986, when the Uruguay Round of trade negotiations was launched.[15] The United States' push for the inclusion of agriculture on the trade agenda is more recent. In both instances, however, the Reagan administration has identified its export interest and has correspondingly cultivated its export lobbies as much as the lobbies have cultivated the administration. Insofar as the vigorous U.S. strategy of opening markets instead of closing them puts these new sectors (which are certainly of enormous actual and potential significance in world trade) on the agenda of freer trade, and insofar as GATT-type principles such as nondiscriminatory MFN treatment for members are the outcome, this strategy has an enormous social benefit: It helps to break down old trade barriers in new sectors while preventing the creation of new trade barriers in old sectors.

15. In view of the strenuous reservations of India, Brazil, and some other developing countries, the compromise solution involved an agreement to conduct the negotiations on services simultaneously with those on goods, but not under GATT formally. See Bhagwati 1987b for an analysis of this procedural matter and its substantive significance.

Unfortunately, this cannot be unambiguously said of the *bilateral* aggressiveness that has also characterized U.S. initiatives to open foreign markets. The capture by protectionists of the countervailing-duty and anti-dumping mechanisms on the import side has its counterpart in the capture of the opening-of-foreign-markets strategy on the export side. Allegations of unfair trade practices afflicting U.S. exports can be made under Section 301 of the U.S. Trade Act, and this section has been used energetically in recent years. The trade legislation now pending before the Congress still has in it silly but dangerous "super-301" provisions aimed at countries in payments surplus and requiring harsh action against these countries.[16]

But such presumptions of unfair trade practices holding up U.S. exports have not merely led to dangerous trade legislation and to an activation of Section 301 cases. They have also contributed to an ethos in which openness of markets and fair access are judged on the basis of "results" rather than by reference to rules. If the desired quantities of exports do not show up, that is taken as sure evidence of inscrutable and unfair protection. In the case of Japan, the complaint usually degenerates further into the question: How much is the United States—not the world—managing to export to Japan in specific sectors?

The actual outcome in this unfair-trade atmosphere, with its bilateral quantity-oriented bias, is likely to degenerate into a replacement of voluntary export restraints on one's imports by what I call "voluntary import expansions" (VIEs)

16. The latest versions are milder than the early Gephardt version, which would have set up a schedule of retaliatory tariffs until the surplus disappeared (as if tariffs could do that). Again, these new versions appear superficially more reasonable in providing retribution only to the extent that the surplus is due to unfair trade practices (as if such a calculation can be meaningful).

of one's exports.[17] Both are departures from the principles of an open trading system, according to which rules matter and quantity outcomes do not. Whereas VERs restrict imports of specific goods from specific countries by getting those countries to adopt export quotas and restraints, VIEs require imports of specific goods by specific countries by all possible means. VERs reflect import-protectionism; VIEs constitute export-protectionism.

There is evidence that those who make U.S. trade policy sometimes fall into the VIE trap, under intense pressure from fair-traders and their allies in the export sectors. In the recent case involving semiconductor chips, the United States had reportedly wished to include in the pact with Japan an assurance that 20 percent of the Japanese market would be supplied by U.S. producers by a target date. Although the formal agreement reportedly did not stipulate this, the informal understanding remained that this figure would provide a way of measuring Japan's fulfillment of its commitment to open its market.[18] The failure of American producers to sell a sufficient amount of chips in Japan despite the pact was a major reason cited in the enactment by the United States of punitive measures against a wide variety of Japanese electronic products in April 1987.

Similarly, the pressure by the United States for the opening of Japan's beef market was aimed at increasing the imports of U.S. beef through larger Japanese quotas, rather than at liberalizing the Japanese import regime (the most likely consequence of which is that Australia would have outcom-

17. See Bhagwati 1987a, Bhagwati and Irwin 1987, and Box 8.6 of *World Development Report* 1987.

18. The formal agreement was concluded *ad referendum* in July 1986, with Japan agreeing to provide "fair and equitable access to its domestic market for foreign semiconductor products." It was formally signed on September 3, 1986.

peted both Japan and the United States). And a 1985 White House press release on the Section 301 case against Japan in regard to quotas on leather and leather footwear states that "Japan has responded to the GATT panel decision by offering to replace the leather quota with tariffs, but the United States has rejected that offer because it would not improve access to the Japanese leather market, and in fact could even further reduce [the U.S.'s] negligible share of the market," thus suggesting that the United States might lose to more competitive suppliers if market access were to be provided through the replacement of a quota with a nondiscriminatory tariff.

Further evidence of such bilateral, trade-diversionary, fix-quantity outcomes replacing genuine opening of foreign markets is found in South Korea's response to bilateral U.S. pressure. Cho (1987) has shown that the final settlement of the Section 301 case regarding South Korea's insurance market did not ease general entry by foreign insurance companies but rather amounted to granting a larger share of the domestic market to two U.S. companies. And when South Korea announced a plan to cut its trade surplus with the United States, there were disturbing reports of trade diversion rather than trade creation from Seoul. The *Financial Times* noted: "South Korea plans to switch almost all its imports of agricultural products, worth $719 million, over the first three-quarters of the year, to the US. Wheat, corn, soybeans and cotton imports formerly bought from countries such as Argentina and China would add about $200 million to the US import bill, officials believe. Imports of parts and raw materials worth about $250 million for the electronics, shipbuilding and steel industries are to be switched from other markets, such as Japan, to the US." (April 27, 1987)

This degeneration of the "harness export interests" approach into fix-quantity, trade-diverting solutions needs to be carefully watched and strenuously resisted. I am somewhat optimistic that the mere act of recognizing it will help trigger a corrective response. In these matters, we can count on assistance from what I call the Dracula Effect: exposing evil to sunlight helps to destroy it. Again, while economists tend to focus on learning by doing, there is also learning before undoing. And those who make U.S. trade policy have shown some resilience and alertness in drawing back from such extreme foolishnesses as the original Gephardt amendment, under which countries running trade surpluses with the United States would have been required to reduce their surpluses on a time schedule or face automatic retaliation. Furthermore, as the United States trade deficit responds to corrective adjustments of the exchange rate, to the prospective reduction of the U.S. budget deficit, and to an expansion of spending by Japan, the exaggerated recent sense that the United States is besieged by unfair foreign traders and the consequent "more open than thou" attitudes that fuel ill-considered bilateral fix-quantity export initiatives should wane.

But if panic is not warranted, neither is complacency. The latest trade bill, in both its Senate version and its House version, still carries evidence of wrongheaded bilateral approaches to the opening of foreign markets. Further purging of these *de facto* protectionist provisions is necessary.

Moreover, there are yet other disturbing signs of a weakened U.S. commitment to most-favored-nation-based multilateralism that may be harder to remedy. One may be of particular significance. I have already remarked the recent reversal of the U.S. position on the use of Article XXIV. Political considerations certainly motivated the agreement with Israel; Destler (1986) notes that the bill had 163 sponsors in the House of Representatives.[19] Political objectives also

19. I recommend Snape's (1987) analysis of trends toward bilateralism in recent U.S. trade policy.

underlie, though to a lesser extent, the recently concluded negotiations for a U.S.-Canada free-trade area. But, as recent writings of Representative Jack Kemp and Senator Phil Gramm only underline, part of the motivation here is certainly the desire to deflect protectionist pressures by pedaling rapidly on any pro-trade bicycle, by chalking up trade-expanding victories that take the political momentum away from the protectionists, and by harnessing directly the export interests of those who would find preferentially protected markets in the countries that would join free-trade areas.[20] The regrettable surrender of the United States on this important front must be ascribed to a short-sighted application of the strategy of harnessing export interests.[21]

I shall turn later to an analysis of the need for improved institutions and for responses to protectionist pressures, and of the need to exploit the opportunity to strengthen the pro-trade forces that are being released by interdependence. Here it should suffice to stress that these new forces are indeed significant. They are also likely to strengthen over time with increased integration and interdependence in the world economy. They give us cause for joy if we are for trade, and for sorrow if we are not.

20. As the U.S. Trade Representative, Ambassador William Brock was reportedly exploring free-trade-area arrangements with any politically agreeable country that might come on board. Such arrangements were allegedly offered to Egypt as well as Israel and discussed with members of the Association of South East Asian Nations.

21. The standard defense of such preferential treatments as the U.S.-Israel and U.S.-Canada free-trade areas—that they leave open the possibility that other nations will join in—does not give enough weight to the strength of trade lobbies, who would object to the entry of new members. The U.S. Congress has not seriously addressed this matter, nor has it systematically analyzed the related matter of the trade-diverting effects of these arrangements.

# Ideology: Example and Ideas

## 5

I ended chapter 4 on an optimistic note, arguing that new pro-trade interests had been created by the increasing interdependence of the world economy and that they should endure and grow. But, as I demonstrated for the remarkable episode of postwar trade liberalization, interests do not work in isolation. I should like to argue now that ideology, in the sense of both example and ideas, also provides grounds for optimism on the part of those who favor freer trade. Once again, in the realms of both example and ideas, there are both pro-protection and pro-trade arguments. However, the pro-trade proponents seem to have the better of it. I will elaborate.

## Example

### Postwar Trade Liberalization

Whereas the post–World War II trade liberalization was driven by the pro-trade bias generated by the negative example of the Smoot-Hawley tariff, today's pro-trade bias can be traced to the positive example of the successful postwar liberalization. And the perception that postwar prosperity was fueled (if not led) by the freeing of trade has greatly strengthened the pro-trade bias inherited from before the Second World War.

---

## The Success of Trade-Liberalizing Developing Countries

The postwar experience has also served to dispel the anti-trade bias that once afflicted policymakers in the developing countries and led to the unusually high reliance on protection that I sketched above. The example that produced this shift in attitudes was the superlative economic performance of those countries (in particular, the Four Tigers[1] of East Asia) that unilaterally liberalized their trade regimes during the 1950s.

This phenomenon is of extraordinary significance. Not only did it demonstrate to developing countries that trade liberalization pays handsome dividends even to a country that, because of its underdevelopment, is presumably somehow beyond the reach of the pro-trade doctrine; in addition, it inevitably generated revisionist reactions addressed to the question whether protection rather than freer trade had been the key to these countries' success.

Let us take a closer look at these issues in the context of the trade policies of the developing countries. We shall then turn to the broader questions they raise—questions that touch directly on the new intellectual developments in the theory of commercial policy.

## The Protectionist Tradition

The intellectual traditions that legitimated the protectionist policies of the developing countries define the pro-protectionist elements that the successful trade liberalization of the Four Tigers helped to contain.

The inward-looking protectionist strategy of policy-

---

1. Taiwan, South Korea, Hong Kong, and Singapore.

---

induced import substitution had four distinct elements, which occurred in various combinations in different developing countries in the 1950s:

• The dominant element was clearly the widespread pessimism concerning the export prospects of the developing countries. Ragnar Nurkse (1959) articulated this pessimism splendidly. The fear was that the growth of the developing countries would require export levels that could not be absorbed by the outside world or by other developing countries. An investment policy of "balanced growth," whereby a country would increasingly have to produce what it wished to consume, would then be dictated by this scenario. Import substitution, assisted by the government, would be both necessary and efficient.[2] This argument does not actually justify blanket protection, but that is essentially what it led to in practice. Because economists are susceptible to the herd instinct, it is not surprising that the writings of many influential development economists of the 1940s and the 1950s reflect pessimism about exports. For instance, Paul Rosenstein-Rodan (1943) argued that investment would not be undertaken by one investor unless it was undertaken simultaneously by others, and that planned coordination of investment, assuring each investor of a market, was therefore necessary. This difficulty, however, would not necessarily arise if there were international markets capable of absorbing

2. In economic jargon: If export pessimism of Nurkse's variety is justified, then the developing countries have monopoly power in trade, and an optimal tariff to exploit it is justified (subject to the qualifications concerning retaliation that I noted in chapter 2). Therefore, a protectionist import-substitution strategy, suitably calibrated, would make sense. Nurkse, having written perceptively about the interwar experience with competitive tariff-making and quantitative restrictions on imports, was not enthusiastic about tariffs; however, his "balanced growth" prescription requires protection as the optimal governmental intervention.

what an investor produced and sold.[3] Raul Prebisch (1952) produced the celebrated and captivating thesis that the primary-product exports of the developing countries faced a long-run decline, and that these countries would therefore have to protect their way into producing manufactures.[4]

• Although export pessimism generated an inward-looking ethos for trade policy, the *coup de grace* to freer trade was delivered, in many cases, from an altogether different direction. Contrary to the expectations of the architects of the International Monetary Fund, who had the interwar experience of knee-jerk competitive devaluations in mind when they stipulated restrictions on exchange-rate changes, the postwar exchange-rate regime turned out to be one of reluctant adjustments. Particularly in much of Latin America, exchange rates were sluggishly adjusted to high inflation rates, causing substantial currency overvaluation with supporting exchange and trade controls. As we now fully appreciate, such overvaluation is tantamount to protection.[5] It also led to blanket, made-to-order "automatic" protection in some developing countries. For instance, in Brazil the "Law of Similars" and in India the principle of "indigenous availability" were utilized to exclude imports, regardless of cost, if domes-

3. Rosenstein-Rodan also used the term "balanced growth," but his argument was altogether different from Nurkse's. Albert Hirschman's (1958) recommendation to induce investment by cutting off imports also fits the pessimism scenario, since the need to cultivate the domestic market arises only if the international markets are not fully and freely accessible (unless an extreme risk aversion to foreign markets is assumed).

4. Strictly speaking, if markets are working well, the mere fact of a long-run decline in the terms of trade would itself move resources into manufactures; no governmental protection to do so would be necessary. Thus, Prebisch's thesis—because its export pessimism was differently premised—had different trade-policy implications than Nurkse's. Nonetheless, it was used to justify import substitution in Latin America, and the attendant protection, in much the same way.

5. See Bhagwati 1986c, appendix.

tic substitutes (however unsuitable or uneconomical) were available; the rationale was that this would "save foreign exchange."[6]

• However, we should not forget that infant-industry protection had a perfectly legitimate role, even within the classical theory of gains from specialization and trade. Yet infant industries do not justify blanket protectionism; besides, promotion (i.e., support through domestic subvention that does not discriminate against foreign trade) rather than protection (which does discriminate against foreign trade) is what is called for. Nonetheless, both the infant-industry argument and the balance-of-payments foreign-exchange-scarcity argument outlined above were accepted indiscriminately, and in GATT Article XVIII(B) they were given international approval.

• Further reinforcement for the idea of broadly protecting infant industries came from the notion that specialization in primary production was politically unacceptable for a modern state. A destiny of "hewers of wood and drawers of water," no matter how advantageous economically, would be at the expense of political status in the international community of nations. (As Oscar Wilde said of the prime example of prosperity through primary production, "There is this world and the next, and then there is New Zealand.") This political preference for industrialization often coexisted with a conviction that manufacturing had considerable externalities—such as creation of a scientific mentality conducive to innovation and technical change—that were not fully reflected in market prices.[7] Whatever the precise mix of the

6. See Bhagwati 1978 and Krueger 1978.

7. Similar convictions underlie, one way or another, the prescriptions of the British "deindustrialization" school (see Kaldor 1966) and the American "manufacturing matters" school (see Cohen and Zysman 1987).

"political status" and "economic externalities" motivations in any specific context, there is little doubt that the developing countries were particularly susceptible to this line of argumentation in the 1950s, when they were both newly independent and heavily specialized in primary production and exports. The historian Edward Carr, writing in 1951, put the argument eloquently:

*What Asia and Africa are fundamentally in revolt against—whatever forms, political or economic, the revolt may take in day-to-day actions—is the nineteenth-century division of the world between advanced and backward peoples and the basis of that division in the intensive industrialization of certain areas of the world to the exclusion of others. Political independence and political equality are no longer enough. These achievements, which seemed all-important so long as they were out of reach, are now seen to be hollow and unreal unless they are backed up by the reality of economic independence and economic equality. . . . The lesson has been thoroughly learned and digested that large-scale modern machine industry confers a high material standard of living and* a widely diffused education and culture, as well as political and military power and prestige. *Backward nations have been transformed into advanced nations through the process of industrialization—and in no other way. . . . Industry is the symbol of progress. Imitation is the last and sincerest form of tribute paid by the colonial East to the industrial West. (p. 94; emphasis added)*

These notions reinforced the other economic arguments that prompted the pursuit of protectionist, import-substitution strategies.

## The Weakened Case for Protectionism

As the postwar period unfolded, the above arguments weakened. The mere fact of industrialization in many developing countries over two decades meant that, at the margin, the pro-industrialization arguments for protection would be less compelling. But far more effective was the demonstration by the trade-liberalizing countries that their superior export performance had led to more successful and substantial industrialization than what the more protectionist nations had managed. By making external markets at least as attractive as home markets, and even by creating a certain pro-export bias by policy design, these countries made their new industries register rapid growth by breaking out of the confines of the smaller domestic markets.

Take the compelling contrast between South Korea and India—prime examples of trade-liberalizing and protectionist regimes. South Korea's manufactured exports, negligible in 1962, amounted by 1980 to nearly four times those of India. South Korea's manufacturing sector was less than 25 percent as large as India's in 1970 (measured in terms of value added); by 1981 it was already up to 60 percent. The contrasts in success with *industrialization*—not just economic growth in general—have been so enormous between the trade-liberalizing and the protectionist countries that the old-fashioned view that protection favors manufacturing in developing countries has lost its appeal.[8]

The main changes, however, were in the demise of the pattern of reluctant exchange-rate adjustment, so that currency overvaluation became a far less serious source of protection. As was demonstrated well (though by no means exclusively) by the Four Tigers, the removal of such anti-export policies and the establishment of a pro-export bias could improve export performance so dramatically that the protection-legitimating export pessimism of Nurkse et al. turned out to have been unwarranted. Indeed, the improve-

8. The older view was based on a static conception according to which primary products were imported and manufactures were exported. However, as industrialization proceeds, protectionist policies confine the new industries to domestic manufactures by creating an anti-export bias.

---

ment in export performance mapped rather well onto better economic performance—a relationship that was especially striking in the case of the Four Tigers but was also corroborated by finer empirical studies of those countries and by time-series analyses of other countries as they moved toward greater trade liberalization through the 1960s and the early 1970s.[9]

The intellectual orthodoxy therefore shifted rather sharply away from the early emphasis on the virtues of protectionism and the attendant import-substitution strategy and toward the merits of trade liberalization and the outward-looking strategy of export promotion.

## The Role of Government

Most of the developing countries that made sustained transitions to more liberal trading regimes do not have *laissez faire* governments. Nor (except for Hong Kong and, perhaps, Singapore) are these free-trade economies that have abandoned protection altogether. For those who seek in the experiences of these economies an endorsement of free trade in the context of a passive government, these facts present obvious difficulties. A careful interpretation of the policy mix in these countries is called for.

In South Korea and Taiwan, neither of which is (like Hong Kong or Singapore) a "city-state" with a natural outward orientation, the shift to the export-promoting strategy took place essentially through a substantial reduction of overvaluation, with a consequent reduction in the degree of protection so afforded, and through the adoption of export incentives that offset and indeed outweighed the residual bias against exports by making the average incentive for exports (i.e., what economists call the *effective exchange rate on exports,*

9. I have in mind principally the OECD, NBER, World Bank, and Kiel Institute projects that I cited in chapter 1.

abbreviated EERx) greater than the average incentive to import (i.e., the *effective exchange rate on imports,* abbreviated EERm). Within this regime, which eliminated the anti-trade bias of the earlier regime (much as an alternative shift to free trade would have done), selectivity of incentives continued to be provided to specific industries. Fully free trade would not have permitted such continued selectivity, nor would it allow the net export incentive (EERx > EERm) of these regimes. Moreover, these policy departures from fully free trade reflected a symbiotic relationship between an active government and the private sector.

Let me offer some stylized explanations of why this combination of policies was productive, considering in turn the net pro-trade bias and the role of government.

The empirical studies of these successful regimes show that they typically involved an explicit endorsement of export promotion by the governments, with subsidies and credit mechanisms geared to that end. Quantification of the subventions shows, however, that they did not result in a substantial excess of incentives to export rather than to sell at home.[10] Now, the theoretical arguments for net export subsidization are well known. For example, for developing countries in particular, there may be externalities to a firm in export markets that are not matched by similar externalities in the domestic market, as when the export markets require investment to promote a product to foreign buyers who are unacquainted with a country's capacity to export this type of good and the returns to this investment then accrue equally to other free-riding potential exporters from that country.[11]

10. In formal terms, the computed excess of EERx over EERm was positive but not large. Indeed, it was substantially less than the reverse excess for the regimes that employed the import-substitution strategy.

11. See Bhagwati 1968 and Mayer 1984. There are also other theoretical arguments for export subsidies; e.g., the optimal tariff structure, as is evi-

But a case for net export subsidization may also be made on the ground that it lends credibility to the government's commitment to the maintenance of a policy framework that protects the export-promotion strategy from random or systematic inroads in the foreseeable future, thus facilitating the investment of resources and entrepreneurial energies in the exploitation of foreign markets. This may well be an important, distinguishing rationale for net export subsidies by developing countries. The role of the government is almost always more manifest there than in developed countries, so that the assurance that a strategy will be protected from disruption by other policy pressures and goals is correspondingly more important.

Perhaps the most compelling case for a framework of export incentives may lie in the beneficial effect that this may exert through the learning by doing and the dynamic economies of scale that are often alleged to characterize protected infant industries. Conventional analyses (e.g. Arrow 1962, Bardhan 1970, Kemp 1966, and Krugman 1984) simply assume that learning accrues from doing, and that markets will not capture fully the benefits of this learning process for firms in protected or promoted infant industries.[12]

dent from Graaff 1949–50 and Feenstra 1986, can include some subsidies, and the Kemp (1966)–Jones (1967) analysis of the optimal mix of capital-flow and trade taxes and subsidies can generate export subsidies in models with international capital mobility. Also, there are arguments for using import tariffs and export subsidies to simulate devaluations and for the use of export subsidies to offset the anti-trade bias in overvalued-exchange-rate regimes (Bhagwati 1968). Hence, it is surprising that economists who have recently been using oligopoly models to produce rationales for export subsidies have asserted that the conventional theory of international trade does not support export subsidization. (See, for instance, the extraordinary statements to that effect by several of the contributors to Krugman 1986.)

12. Krugman (1984) concentrates, rather, on how such protection, with scale economies, can lead to the firm's eventually exporting. Basevi (1970) and Pomfret (1975) did similarly. I have shown (Bhagwati 1986d) that such

On the other hand, the developing countries are witness to countless cases of firms and industries that did not grow out of protection-fed infancy. The problem lies in the foolish assumption that learning *automatically* follows from doing. As anyone who has taught should know, students can repeat courses and get nowhere. The Soviets have produced countless Ladas which you and I can happily do without. Rather, learning is a function of doing *within an appropriate environment*. The contrast between the sheltered-home-market environment created by protectionism and the internationalized environment imposed by a pro-trade bias is the real key to differential outcomes of the learning process.

The learning-by-doing school of protectionism comes up with the wrong prescription because its key assumption rests on an erroneous premise. The assumption that a firm inevitably learns by doing, no matter what, must be firmly rejected. In urging this, I am reminded of Thomas Balogh's advice to me on how to debate Milton Friedman: "As soon as Friedman says, 'let us assume this,' stop him and say: 'no, I do *not* assume that.' For, if you let him assume what he wants, you will be landed with consequences you do not like." In this instance, the consequences are not necessarily disagreeable, but they almost certainly will encourage folly and cause harm.

This brings us to the more general question of the role of government in the successful Far Eastern countries. These countries—including Japan—have highly energetic and involved governments, as has long been known to students of

a paradoxical phenomenon can exist *without invoking scale economies,* building exclusively on the fact that protection permits price discrimination by the protected domestic monopolist and leads to exports whereas free trade would have destroyed the monopoly and led to imports. My case, which is welfare-worsening for sure, is far more prevalent in many developing countries, and possibly elsewhere too, than the more sanguine possibility reflecting scale economies that Krugman has noted.

trade and of payment regimes.[13] This is not to deny that some have believed otherwise. For example, in one segment of "Free to Choose," Milton Friedman characterized Japan as an example of the superiority of the market over government. As a member of the panel on the program, I remarked that the visible hand in Japan might be invisible to him but was certainly not so to the Japanese. But Friedman can be forgiven for self-indulgence toward his economic beliefs; we are all prey to that in varying degrees. After all, how could an economic miracle have occurred if the policymakers had not followed our preferred policies? Recalling that public goods have the property that I can enjoy them without depriving you of your pleasure, I have formulated the following law: Economic miracles are a public good; each economist sees in them a vindication of his pet theories.

The key question is not whether there is governmental action in the Far Eastern economies, but rather how these successful economies have managed their intervention and their strategic decisionmaking better than the unsuccessful economies. This is a complex question, but some stylized answers can nonetheless be attempted.

An important aspect of the difference in behavior of governments toward the private sector seems to be that the Far Eastern governments, by and large, issue *prescriptions* rather than *proscriptions* (Bhagwati 1978, chapter 8), whereas countries such as India do the opposite. The governments of "dos" generally produce economic performance superior to that produced by governments of "don'ts." There are two reasons why this might be so.

First, although a prescriptive government may prescribe as badly as a proscriptive government proscribes, a proscrip-

13. See, e.g., chapter 8 of Bhagwati 1978.

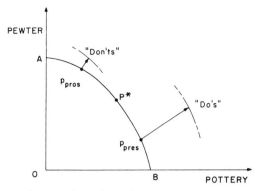

Figure 10   The stifling effect. Proscriptive governments stifle initiative more than prescriptive ones, causing production possibilities to expand less rapidly.

tive government will tend to stifle initiative, whereas a prescriptive government will tend to leave open areas (outside of the prescriptions) where initiative can be exercised. Thus, even though each government might distort allocation of existing resources equally, the proscriptive government will tend to stifle technical change and entrepreneurial activity and hence hurt growth. This is illustrated by figure 10, where $OAB$ is the set of production possibilities. (Imagine that only pewter and pottery can be made from given resources and technology.) $P^*$ is the optimal outcome. If government activity distorts the economy away from $P^*$, the proscriptive government distorts it to $p_{pros}$ whereas the prescriptive government distorts it to $p_{pres}$. However, the latter permits rapid expansion of the production-possibility set. Productive forces grow faster, owing to less stifling of initiatives, and this allows people to do things other than the prescribed ones. As the arrows show, there is a greater *stifling effect* under the proscriptive regime.

Second, under proscriptive governments, entrepreneurs

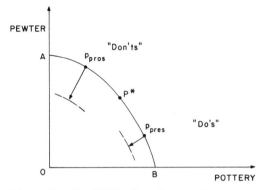

Figure 11   The DUP effect. Proscriptive governments induce more DUP activities than prescriptive ones, causing production possibilities to shrink more from wasteful use of resources.

tend to evade the proscriptions by diverting resources into unproductive ways of making income.[14] In contrast, prescriptive governments provide fewer inducements for such unproductive activities, because the prescriptions leave large areas open for initiatives. Note that in figure 11 the $p_{pros}$ distortion leads to a greater shift *inside* the current production-possibility set. The *DUP effect* hurts the proscriptive government disproportionately.

Proscriptive governments are more likely to be adversarial to private entrepreneurship; the bureaucrats and the politicians are in the driver's seat. Prescriptive governments, in contrast, appear to work in a symbiotic relationship with private entrepreneurs. Japan and India provide two well-known illustrations of this contrast. The relationship between MITI and the Japanese firms is intimate, whereas that in India between the planners and the private entrepreneurs is not. Symbiosis between a government and private entrepreneurs can have two favorable effects. First, when engaging in plan-

14. These are known as *directly unproductive profit-seeking* (DUP) activities. (See note 18 below.)

ning for a particular industry, the government can make use of the entrepreneurs' familiarity with the industry—know-how that cannot otherwise be obtained by bureaucrats. Second, the symbiosis can reinforce the credibility of the government's commitment to an economic strategy such as outward orientation. With MITI agreeing to a projected or planned economic scenario, the government can be expected to adhere to a supportive policy mode rather than a disruptive one.

*First versus Second Pessimism*

There can be no question about the role played by the success of the Far Eastern economies in converting intellectual opinion in the developing countries to an appreciation of the benefits of outward orientation—and hence predisposing them toward unilateral initiatives to liberalize their highly protective external trade-and-payment regimes. These success stories demonstrated the fallacy of the "first pessimism" of the 1950s, which reflected the view that markets could not be found for increasing exports because of natural external constraints. But now, in the 1980s, there is evidence of a new pessimism.

The "second pessimism" is based not on the view that markets do not exist, but rather on the gloomy assessment that protectionism will close markets once one has entered them.[15] This view, unless one takes the extreme position so that *any* expansion of exports will lead to restrictive trade constraints and hence justify a comprehensive shift to what Nurkse called "balanced growth," requires a calibrated response. The implied lack of markets abroad in sectors where such protectionism is likely to materialize will suggest protectionist prudence by the exporter in these sectors alone,

---

15. The contrast between these two pessimisms is defined and analyzed in Bhagwati 1986c. See also Bhagwati, Krueger, and Snape 1987.

exactly as in John Stuart Mill's argument for a monopoly-power-in-trade tariff.

If, however, my assessment in chapter 4 is correct, there is reason for hope that the second pessimism will be invalidated, as the first pessimism was. And whereas the first pessimism reflected a gloomy assessment of *market forces,* so that the only option was to adjust to it through balanced growth, the second pessimism is *man-made.* It can therefore be remedied by human action. The governments of the trading countries can act to contain protectionism and maintain a freer trading system.

## Ideas

As it happened, analyses of trade policies of the developing countries and of their differential performance (and other empirical observations) gave the recent developments in the theory of commercial policy their impetus. Economics at its best responds to empirical reality and puzzles, and here it did just that.

Interestingly, however, these developments have gone in two different directions, one enriching the anti-protectionist presumptions and the other enlarging the scope of beneficial trade intervention. The former theoretical breakthrough concerns the growing analysis of unproductive activities and their integration into the theoretical framework of political economy; the latter relates to the growth of imperfectly competitive (in particular, small-group oligopoly) models. The former primarily suggests that the conventional analyses of the cost of protection have ignored the associated costs of the unproductive activities to which protection gives rise. The latter, by introducing imperfections in the market, suggests that the possibilities of welfare-improving trade intervention highlighted in conventional competitive analyses are also understated.

---

## DUP Activities

The possibilities of widespread growth of resource-using unproductive activities, such as tariff evasion and lobbying for the procurement of lucrative import and investment licenses, were evident and important in many of the developing countries that were examined during the late 1960s. This led to the development of new theoretical analyses of these phenomena, to Krueger's (1974) development of the concept of *rent-seeking* to characterize lobbying for the premia (rents, in economic jargon) that quotas create and fetch, and to my development of the broader concept of *directly unproductive profit-seeking (DUP) activities* (Bhagwati 1982b).[16]

Thus, to the conventional "deadweight" loss, which protection causes by distorting production and consumption decisions, international economists now typically add an estimate of the lobbying costs that are likely to attend on seeking or securing import licenses and the like. However, the early presumptions of DUP theorists that these added costs would be extremely large have now given way to more modest expectations. There are at least two reasons for this. First, the earliest estimates—particularly those of Krueger (1974)—were based on the assumption that rent-seeking would lead to market-value losses as large as the rents being sought: a dollar lost for a dollar chased. This presupposes open competition among risk-neutral lobbyists. But in reality the "brother-in-

---

16. See the extensive review and synthesis of this literature in Bhagwati 1982b. The relationship between rent-seeking and DUP activities is explained in Bhagwati 1982b and in Bhagwati 1983. Tullock 1967 is a landmark in DUP theory; see also Colander 1984.

---

law theorem" often applies: Favored lobbyists usually have a better chance than the others of getting the license and the rent it fetches, and this deters others from expending as many resources on rent-seeking as perfect competition would imply.[17] Second, as T. N. Srinivasan and I have emphasized, market losses are not necessarily social losses. If import quotas have strongly distorted domestic allocation of resources to begin with, the market price of a dollar's worth of resources diverted to rent-seeking aimed at the import quotas is not its true social cost at all. In fact, in "highly distorted" economies such resource diversion, while directly unproductive, may paradoxically improve welfare (see, in particular, Bhagwati and Srinivasan 1980). In jargon, the shadow or social cost of productive factors withdrawn from productive use into DUP activities could be negative.[18] Although there are countless such observations of "value subtraction" in productive activities, when social costs and values rather than market prices are used to make estimates, this is undoubtedly an extreme phenomenon. Suffice it to say that the social cost of rent-seeking is likely, in distorted economies, to be below its nominal, market cost. But, with both these caveats duly noted, this literature does strengthen the anti-protectionist hand.

17. In turn, this presumption must be qualified somewhat: Becoming a favored lobbyist may require the expenditure of resources.

18. Theoretically, this observation is of profound importance, for it means that—contrary to the practice of James Buchanan (1980) and many others of the public-choice school—it is not meaningful to define unproductive activities as necessarily welfare-worsening. This is why the adjective *directly* is used to qualify those unproductive profit-seeking activities, since (indirectly or ultimately) they may improve welfare. Hence, I use the term *DUP activities* to describe the generic set of activities that use resources and produce income but zero output. On these questions—which affect critically the untenable equation of direct and ultimate waste in both the works of the public-choice school and the long-standing discussions (since Adam Smith and Karl Marx) of the concept of unproductive labor and activities—see Bhagwati 1980, 1982b, 1983.

## Increasing Returns, Market Structure, and Strategic Trade Policy

On the other hand, the development of the theory of international trade in the direction of models with imperfect competition (resulting from increasing returns to scale of production) has pushed the scientific frontier in the opposite direction.

At first blush this is paradoxical, since the primary way in which analysts of developing countries' trade policies have considered increasing returns to scale has been by arguing that protectionist policies, by stimulating production for the small domestic market, would impose large losses owing to the small scale of production. Further, by making domestic monopoly possible—whereas free trade would have destroyed this monopoly—protection would lead to conventional efficiency losses, and possibly to X-efficiency (i.e., "goofing-off") losses too. In this frame of thinking, the economies of scale are large in the context of the domestic market but are not large relative to the world market; they matter only (and then adversely) when protection makes them pertinent; under free trade they are of no consequence. I have little doubt that this is a reasonable approximation to the reality of many developing countries and many industries in all countries. It only underlines the case for free trade.

However, in the recent theoretical work of economists studying small-group market structure and its impact on commercial policy, it is assumed that economies of scale are large relative to world markets, and that they result in an oligopolistic market structure.[19] High-technology, knowl-

---

19. I have in mind here many authors, including James Brander, Barbara Spencer, Gene Grossman, Jonathan Eaton, James Markusen, Antony Venables, Paul Krugman, and Avinash Dixit. See the survey by Dixit (1983) and the synthesis by Eaton and Grossman (1986).

---

edge-intensive industries are generally presumed by these theorists to conform to this structure. In these cases, evidently, prices do not generally reflect social costs, either at home or in foreign trade. But although free trade under these circumstances is not (generally speaking) optimal, the problem is that the precise nature of the intervention to be used depends critically on the nature of the strategic interaction between the oligopolistic firms. Consider the highly simplified model (due originally to Brander and Spencer [1981]) in which one domestic firm and one foreign firm produce a homogeneous product only for a third country, where they compete. Here, an export subsidy is socially optimal if the firms follow the Cournot-Nash strategy, by which each firm selects its optimal level of output taking the output of the rival as given. But if in the very same model we assume that, rather than choosing output levels and letting prices adjust correspondingly, the firms engage in the Bertrand strategy of setting prices and letting outputs adjust to the demands at those prices, then the prescription for intervention is not an export subsidy but an export tax (see Eaton and Grossman 1986). In each case the intervention shifts the above-normal profits to the domestic firm and hence increases the national welfare.[20]

This sensitivity (or lack of robustness) of policy interventions to assumptions about the nature of oligopolistic strategic interaction creates information requirements for

20. An analogy with the monopoly-power-in-trade argument is apt. In that argument, monopoly power is not perceived by the firm that acts competitively, and the government intervenes with an optimal tariff that exploits this unperceived and neglected monopoly power. In the present instance, the firm cannot credibly move away from its reaction curve toward the maximal-profit, optimal-welfare output or price decision, and the government must intervene to shift the firm's reaction curve so that this maximal-profit output or price gets onto it.

policy intervention that appear to many of the architects of this theoretical innovation to be sufficiently intimidating to suggest that policymakers had better leave it alone.[21] This viewpoint is reinforced for them by doubts as to whether there are indeed (excess) profits to be shifted through such intervention. Grossman (1986, p. 57) has put it cogently:

*Often what appears to be an especially high rate of profit is just a return to some earlier, risky investment. Research and development expenses, for example, can be quite large, and many ventures end in failure. Firms will only undertake these large investments if they can reap the benefits in those instances where they succeed. Once the market is in operation, we will of course only observe those companies that have succeeded. We may then be tempted to conclude that profit rates are unusually high. But industry profits should be measured inclusive of the losses of those who never make it to the marketing stage.*

The practical application of the new and theoretically valid increasing-returns-based argument for policy intervention to shift profits toward oneself in oligopolistic industries is, therefore, beset with difficulties. These are further compounded, as was the classical theoretical prescription for an optimal tariff, by the fact that the new case for export subsidization or import tariffs[22] is based on considerations of *national*

21. There are informational requirements, to be sure, when conventional interventions for market failure are recommended. In this instance, however, we need information on behavioral assumptions, which seem harder to track down. Attempts by Spencer (1986), Rodrik (1987), and others to provide guidelines or rules of thumb for meaningful inferences of this kind are interesting but not persuasive.

22. Import tariffs can also shift profits, while gaining for the protected industry economies of scale that give it a competitive advantage over the foreign firms that are then denied access to this segment of the world market. See Krugman 1984.

advantage and presupposes that foreign governments do not retaliate.[23]

As with the unilateral exercise of an optimal tariff to exploit monopoly power in trade, the asymmetric, unilateral use by a government of export subsidies or import tariffs in oligopolistic industries to gain a competitive edge and possibly shift profits to the country's advantage is, however, likely to invite retaliation from aggrieved trading partners.

Such retaliation is likely in precisely the knowledge-intensive high-technology industries, in which economies of scale relative to world markets are presumed to be significant. These industries are widely regarded as important in themselves. Locating them behind one's own borders is often seen as a matter of securing broader political and economic benefits, just as manufacturing was so regarded by developing countries during the postwar years. Intervention by foreign governments, regardless of whether profit-shifting-related advantages exist or not, is generally seen, therefore, as an attempt to get a larger share of this important pie than is warranted by legitimate market forces. This is surely a major reason behind the sensitivity in the United States on this question, which leads to allegations of asymmetrical, predatory governmental interventions in such industries by Japan and to demands for retaliation.

If retaliation occurs, then it is not beyond the ingenuity of economists to construct cases in which it would still leave the country that had initiated the profit-shifting game better off. But, as with the earlier retaliation analysis of the optimal tariff for exploiting monopoly power, the competitive, retaliatory policies provoked by attempts at profit-shifting are likely to leave each country worse off, especially if such ac-

23. Strategic interaction is entirely confined to governments in conventional analysis, because firms are competitive. It is at both the firm level and the government level when firms are oligopolistic.

tions spill over into other areas of trade policy or drag other players into the game simply because of the multilateral aspects of international trade.

To shift the perspective: Should such retaliation be encouraged, or even embodied in national trade-policy rules? This is recommended by some (e.g. Krasner and Goldstein [1984]) who build on Axelrod's (1981) celebrated advocacy of a "tit for tat" strategy for inducing nonpredatory, cooperative behavior (after repeated games) by recalcitrant game players. Under this strategy, the United States would play fair on the first move and would then retaliate if Japan were to follow with a predatory move; subsequently, the United States would match Japan's moves. The problems with applying such strategies to trade policy are legion, and they show the irrelevance of the Axelrod prescription. In particular, bilateral determination of the other player's fairness may be confidently expected to lean toward being self-serving—what is tit and what is tat becomes problematic and contentious. A tat, unfairly alleged and retaliated against with a tit, will invite resentment and will probably generate trade skirmishes rather than lead down the benign cooperative route that Axelrod conjures up. Indeed, in a protectionist climate such as today's, tats are likely to be found readily and charged against successful rivals, and the Axelrod strategy is likely to be captured by those who seek export protectionism through voluntary import expansions.[24]

For these reasons, I am strongly opposed to strategic trade-policy-making, whether the intention is to shift profits

---

24. For a useful analysis of other limitations of the Axelrod strategy, see Brander 1985. I should emphasize that the Axelrod strategy, as originally analyzed, works with two players who are as long-lived as the repeated games they play, whereas trade typically involves more than two players and, in democracies in particular, the players change with changes in governments and in bureaucracies.

---

to oneself or to retaliate against rivals who are allegedly doing so. However, the problems and pressures raised by such fears and allegations require that the institutions governing trade policy be supplemented by procedures aimed at ensuring a *broad* balance of advantages from artificial subventions in a *limited* number of high-technology industries where significant scale economies relative to world markets can be plausibly established as important. I shall return to this question later, emphasizing that these procedures should be multilateral.

## The "Manufacturing Matters" Muddle

At this point it is necessary to address and dismiss those who have recently advocated trade-policy interventions on the ground that "manufacturing matters." A number of different fallacies underlie the pro-manufacturing arguments that have surfaced and have fed protectionism.

• The most influential argument, which long predates the recent U.S. concerns about deindustrialization, came from Nicholas Kaldor (1966) and his colleagues at the Cambridge Department of Applied Economics.[25] The core of Kaldor's argument was that the progressive British shift out of manufactures into services was economically harmful because services were technically stagnant whereas manufactures were characterized by substantial technical change, and that this required state intervention to protect manufactures. Kaldor even managed even to get the Chancellor of the Exchequer, James Callaghan, to enact the (now repealed) Selective Em-

25. Adjustment pressures on British industry predated those on American industries, producing this differential timing of their deindustrialization schools. Another contrast is that the British school was led by distinguished economists such as Kaldor, whereas the American school has been made up of political scientists, sociologists, and economic journalists.

ployment Tax, which taxed employment in the service industries with a view to shifting labor into the manufacturing industries.

The problem with Kaldor's argument was the notion that services were technically stagnant. His view was undoubtedly formed by the empirical reality of the traditional British service sector, exemplified by the post office and the mom-and-pop retail stores outside Oxbridge Colleges. This has no counterpart in today's service sector, where technical progress is rapid and more striking than in many manufactures.

• There is also the related and frequently held presumption that manufactures generate beneficial externalities which other sectors do not. This goes back to earlier controversies over the merits of industrialization, such as the arguments that attended the early American debate on manufactures. Consider, for example, the following (quoted in Folsom and Lubar 1980 on the pages cited):

*The introduction of manufactures would extend knowledge of all kinds, particularly scientifical. The elements of natural philosophy and of chemistry, now form an indispensable branch of education among the manufacturers of England. They cannot get on without it. They cannot understand or keep pace with the daily improvements of manufacture without scientific knowledge. (page 190)*

*There is another point of importance, in reference to manufactures, which ought not to be omitted in this connection, and it is this—that in addition to what may be called their direct operation and influence, manufactures are a great school for all the practical arts. As they are aided themselves, in the progress of inventive sagacity, by hints and materials from every art and every science, and every kingdom of nature, so, in their turn, they create the skill and furnish the instruments for carrying on almost all the other pursuits. Whatever pertains to machinery, in all the great branches of industry, will probably be found to have its origin, directly or indirectly, in that skill which can be acquired only in connection with manufactures. (pages 289–290)*

Whatever merit this line of argument may have had when manufactures were being compared with agriculture, it has surely no validity when manufactures are compared with modern services.

• Manufactures have even been considered character-forming, as in the following lines of nineteenth-century American verse:

*From industry the sinews strength acquire,*
*The limbs expand, the bosom feels new fire.*
*Unwearied industry pervades the whole,*
*Nor lends more force to body than to soul.*

*Hence character is form'd, and hence proceeds*
*Th' enlivening heat that fires to daring deeds:*
*Then animation bids the spirit warm,*
*Soar in the whirlwind and enjoy the storm.*
*(quoted: Folsom and Lubar 1980, p. 138)*

But such sentiments have been expressed in defense of every sector for which protection has been sought. (Agriculture in developed countries and services in developing countries have been the principal beneficiaries of such special pleas.)

• The proponents of manufactures have even suggested that pride and honor require a country to manufacture what it uses and consumes. Matching the occasional exhortation that a self-respecting country must grow its own food, the advocates of manufactures have often been animated by sentiments such as the following, expressed in 1808:

*Is it not a reflection that even the* flag of our country, *is made of Foreign manufacture, and our legislators and patriots, while delivering the most dignified and national sentiments, are clothed in the*

*produce of a foreign land? It is—We shall ever bear a secondary*
*grade, in the rank of nations, if we are not independent of all. We*
*shall ever feel our insignificance, if we are dependent on others for*
*what we most want, and what we can best supply. (quoted: Folsom*
*and Lubar 1980, p. 154)*

Nothing bothers the proponents of pride in national production of manufactures so much as their fellow nationals who
break ranks and buy foreign goods. The "Buy American"
slogans of today are simply a latter-day manifestation of the
spirit embodied in the following lines of early American
verse:

*Shall we, of gewgaws gleaning half the globe,*
*Disgrace our country with a foreign robe?*
*Forbid it int'rest, independence, shame,*
*And blush that kindles bright at honour's flame!*

*Should peace, like sorcery, with her spells controul*
*Our innate springs and energies of soul;*
*To you, Columbian dames! my accents call,*
*Oh, save your country from the threaten'd fall!*
*Will ye, blest fair! adopt from every zone*
*Fantastic fashions, noxious in your own?*
*At wintry balls in gauzy garments drest,*
*Admit the dire destroyer in your breast?*
*(quoted: Folsom and Lubar 1980, p. 138)*

• The modern American enthusiasts of manufactures have
developed yet another innovative argument. According to
Cohen and Zysman (1987, chapter 2), having manufactures is
critical because a shift to modern services without local
manufacturing is improbable and perhaps impossible. Economists, according to these gentlemen, are in error when they
argue as if the decline of manufacturing and the rise of services can be contemplated; linkages between the two make

this a contradiction.[26] Let me quote them lest anyone think I am offering a straw man:

*There are . . . other kinds of linkages in the economy, such as those which tie the crop duster to the cotton fields, the ketchup maker to the tomato patch, the wine press to the vineyards (to return to our focus on agriculture [as a parallel]). Here the linkages are tight and quite concrete . . . the linkage is a bind, not a junction or substitution point. Offshore the tomato farm and you close or offshore the ketchup plant. No two ways about it.*

Now, as I read the profound assertion about the tomato farm and the ketchup plant, I was eating my favorite Crabtree & Evelyn vintage marmalade. It surely had not occurred to me that England grew its own oranges.

These fallacies have acquired greater appeal in recent years in the industrialized countries, for reasons that were explained in chapter 4. The awareness that similar fallacies have occurred in earlier periods, and that many of their premises have been flawed, should help to contain their pernicious influence. But this brings me to my final theme: How should our institutions be adapted, in light of the evolving trends in interests and ideas, so that the impact of the forces of protection is weakened and the new anti-protection forces are strengthened and given greater play?

26. Zysman and Cohen—who appear not to have been familiar with the older and more influential English school of deindustrialization worriers—assume complementarity between services and manufactures, whereas the English school assumes substitution between them. Starting from opposed premises, the two schools manage nonetheless to leave their adherents with identical fears.

# Institutional Reform

## 6

The analysis of recent protectionism and the prognosis of future trends, as defined by both interests and ideology, suggest several institutional changes, small and large, that would aid the forces favoring freer trade and would inhibit, impede, and deflect the protagonists of protection. Let me first outline two broad areas of reform and then sketch certain "areas of understanding" where more enlightened comprehension and appreciation of trade-policy questions will be needed if vulnerability to protectionist pressures is to be avoided.

## Institutional Change: Balancing Interests Better

The need for institutional changes that will give more play to the forces favoring freer trade and will permit the costs of protection to weigh more adequately in the deliberations than they now do is evident. The pro-protectionism bias of the current institutions needs to be corrected. Let me suggest some possibilities.

• To minimize the capture of the anti-dumping and countervailing-duty mechanisms by protectionists for the purposes of harassment and trade restriction, it would be useful to work toward more impartial institutional procedures by having bilateral or (preferably) multilateral panels investigate the complaints, by permitting the imposition of penalties on petitioners whose complaints are adjudicated to have been frivolous and to have been intended only for harassment, and by setting a much higher threshold before relief will be granted (for example, no relief would be provided in a countervailing-duty case unless the foreign subsidy were to exceed, say, 20 percent, rather than the minuscule amounts now being countervailed).

At the same time, differential and adverse treatment of foreign suppliers' trading practices relative to one's own, and deliberately restrictive interpretations of the "unfairness" of legitimate trading practices, need to be institutionally documented on a regular basis so as to ensure greater transparency and hence possible reform through enlightenment and embarrassment.

• The current institutional procedures for safeguards actions, where market injury is a precondition for possible relief, are geared entirely to allowing an industry seeking relief to establish injury. The offsetting impact of the proposed relief on consumers and other interests emerges therefore only at later stages of the process, if at all. If the economic costs of protection and the political benefits of granting relief could be considered at the same time, this would ensure that the two interests would be more properly balanced in the public perception and in the policy process. Indeed, by making the institutional process build into itself the cost of protection, we would be remedying the "free rider" problem that generally inhibits consumers from organizing to make their interests effective; the institutions would ensure that consumers' interests would be reflected in the process, whether they were lobbied for or not. There is much to be said, therefore, in favor of institutionalizing, at the outset of safeguards investigations, calculations such as the estimated cost to consumers of preserving a job in the protected industry.[1,2]

• But it is not enough to reflect these costs of protection in the decision-making process so as to achieve a better balance of the conflicting interests over protection of specific industries and firms. It is also desirable, in certain cases where relief is granted through protection and leads to continued viability of the industry, to eventually charge part of that cost to the industry.[3] In the celebrated Chrysler bailout, the effective cost of raising the financing was reduced by a governmental loan guarantee. The voluntary export restraints that also helped Chrysler and its domestic rivals may have cost American consumers about a billion dollars during 1983 alone.[4] When Chrysler eventually landed on its feet, and so did General Motors and other companies, the triumphant chief executive officers awarded themselves big bonuses, hugely rewarding themselves for their turnaround and roundly ignoring the societal costs. Should not these hidden costs have been recovered from these firms (at least in part) before the bonuses were distributed? Clearly, some institutionalization of repayment to the exchequer of the social costs incurred by protection in such cases should be a leading item on the reform agenda.

1. In 1983 the cost of preserving the job of one British auto worker with quotas on the importing of automobiles was the equivalent of the wages of four British industrial workers (see *World Development Report* 1987, figure 8.4).

2. Finger (1982) suggested that countries be encouraged to publicize to their trading partners' citizens the costs of their partners' trade policies. "The Argentines," he wrote, "would buy television time in Japan to show an Argentine family enjoying a big roast beef and to show Japanese families how much of that roast beef they would have after the government of Japan took its slice" (p. 376).

3. Willett (1984) expresses similar concerns.

4. This estimate is from Tarr and Morkre 1984.

## Institutional Change: Adjustment Assistance

An equally urgent reform in the institutional setup is the embrace of adjustment-assistance programs, not just unilaterally but also via multilateral reform of the part of Article XIX that pertains to safeguards.

As I emphasized in chapter 4, not only has the increased globalization of the world economy created new pro-trade interests; in addition, the traditional protectionist responses to significant import pressure in a sector have been contained somewhat by new alternatives, such as the outmigration of firms. Thus, firms often move abroad rather than clamor for protection at home. But when a firm threatens to move abroad (and especially when the firm is large and the community is small), the protectionist pressures are likely to spill over into an increased clamor from the workers threatened with layoffs and from wider groups within the community, leading to pressure to close the foreign-investment option.

It is therefore necessary to create institutional support mechanisms to ease the consequences of, and hence to facilitate, the decline and exit of firms in the context of the vastly more integrated world economy. Adjustment-assistance programs, aimed at this task, are more critical now than ever.

It is tempting to argue that assistance for import-competition-affected adjustment is unreasonable and inefficient, that all changes require adjustment, and that assistance should be provided in a generic fashion for all kinds of changes rather than just for import-related changes. This viewpoint is valid in a cosmopolitan world that does not differentiate between foreign and domestic communities. However, in the real world the refusal to accept change—and hence the need to accommodate to it and facilitate it through adjustment assistance—is greater when the source of the disturbance is presumed to be foreign. If you import cheap steel and I lose my job in Pennsylvania, that is not quite the same as if I lose my job because you build a steel mill in California; it leads to greater resentment and more resistance to change. The case for differential adjustment assistance rests on this asymmetry in communities' attitudes toward change from foreign and domestic sources.

It is logical, therefore, to combine temporary protection (afforded under safeguards measures) with adjustment assistance (such as retraining programs for workers). In view of the budgetary constraints that now afflict most governments (and certainly that of the United States), an attractive and feasible way to do this may be to integrate the revenues that arise from the use of tariffs to provide temporary protection with the financing of the adjustment assistance in a "closed loop,"[5] so that, while one hand provides respite, the other encourages exit.

A policy proposal that would mix three elements is worthy of consideration: (1) Instead of voluntary export restrictions, the safeguard action would use the nondiscriminatory tariff as contemplated in Article XIX. (2) The revenues generated by the tariff would be used to finance adjustment assistance, possibly through a common fund receiving all such tariff revenues. (3) The protective tariff would be explicitly set on a declining time-bound schedule.[6]

Such a policy mix has the potential to provide a viable and attractive alternative to the voluntary-export-restriction

5. The "closed loop" idea, introduced in Feenstra and Bhagwati 1982 in the context of import competition and response thereto, is discussed in relation to adjustment assistance in Bhagwati 1982c (chapter 1).

6. Elements of such a policy mix are combined imaginatively, with the U.S. scene in view, in two independent contributions by Lawrence and Litan (1986) and Hufbauer and Rosen (1986).

regime that proliferated in the 1970s, and thus to keep the trade regime from drifting into Jan Tumlir's dystopia of a fix-quantity, discriminatory nightmare (see Tumlir 1985). A policy incorporating these elements would restore nondiscrimination (in using tariffs rather than VERs) and would ensure that the safeguard protection would be transparent and temporary.

Could such a policy be a worthy replacement for Article XIX, which has fallen into disuse? I believe that it has possibilities, and that they can be explored and exploited in the Uruguay Round. It offers both exporting and importing countries something. In taking back from exporting countries the very large rents that VERs fetch in some cases, it offers the importing countries a definite advantage. The revenues contributed to adjustment-assistance programs represent another advantage for the importing countries. For the exporting countries, the loss of rents (or, in case of the "porous-protection" model, the loss of the alternative advantages discussed in chapter 3) is compensated for by the fact that the protection will be temporary and by the fact that the chances of its being reimposed are reduced by the mounting of the adjustment-assistance program. If the reform were to bring a return to the GATT-based nondiscriminatory mode of safeguards, that in itself would be a major gain for many of the countries—among them the developing counties—that fear they will become the selected targets of a discriminatory imposition of voluntary export restrictions.[7]

---

7. The above proposal for Article XIX reform is very different from the often-made proposal to weaken the article so as to legitimate selective, discriminatory imposition of safeguards protection. I agree fully with the objections raised by Hindley (1987) to this latter option; it would simply institutionalize VERs, for the apparent benefit of surveillance, and thus perpetuate their use by giving them the virtue of legitimacy.

## Areas of Understanding

The institutional changes discussed above can strengthen the political forces that oppose protectionism by incorporating the cost of protection in the institutional processes so as to achieve a better balance of interests, and by facilitating adjustment and correspondingly defusing protectionist responses. But there is also a need to address the danger posed by inadequate thinking on several issues that have recently been the subjects of extensive concern and thoughtless action that plays into the hands of protectionist forces. The powerful political and psychological concern that these issues inspire cannot be wished away. Rather, what can and should be done is to clarify the issues, to try to allay the underlying fears, and (if need be) to suggest alternative policies that will be less damaging to a liberal trading regime than those now being advocated.

---

*Trade Policy and the Assignment Problem: Workers' Rights, etc.*

One important issue arises from the incessant tendency to make restrictive trade policy a handmaiden of loftier objectives. A typical example is provided by the linkage established between trade access to the United States on a most-favored-nation basis by the Soviet Union and the latter's performance with regard to the emigration of Jews and human rights in general. I suspect that it is precisely to rid itself eventually of such linkages that the Soviet Union aspires to join GATT. Membership in GATT would help to secure MFN rights without the intrusion of political tradeoffs.[8] In

---

8. This is not to say that the U.S. could not invoke Article XXXV at the time of the USSR's admission to GATT membership. This would enable the U.S. to negotiate the specific GATT obligations that the U.S. would undertake with respect to the USSR. For discussions of other issues raised by the USSR's interest in joining GATT, see Dirksen 1987 and Kennedy 1987.

---

fact, it would do so without the Soviet Union's having to undertake reciprocal market-access obligations, since there is no meaningful way in which any foreign trader can enter the Soviet market (or the market of any other centrally planned Communist state) at any given level of tariff restrictions, selling what it will and buying freely what it wants.[9] In trade between a primarily rules-based economy and a mainly quantity-based economy, GATT-protected access binds the former but cannot bind the latter. Links between trade access and issues such as human rights are easy to justify in situations where trade is basically not governed by trade rules and a rules-based regime to begin with. But where using trade for such objectives can conflict with the maintenance of a desirable trade regime, the question must be raised: Are there no better, less costly policies that might achieve these objectives?

The political scientist David Baldwin (1986) has properly reminded us that we must ask not whether economic embargoes are effective, but whether they are less ineffective than alternative policy instruments in achieving the political goals that the embargoes are designed to serve. I would like to turn this around and say that although trade policy may be utilized to serve a particular political or social objective, it may be more cost-effective to use *another* policy or set of policies toward that purpose and to keep trade policy within the bounds of an international regime that secures gains from trade. In the words of Nobel laureate Jan Tinbergen, this becomes then a "policy assignment" problem; the relevant answer may well be to use trade policy to secure gains from trade and to use other policies for objectives such as human rights.

This question is particularly pertinent to the movement

9. The only reciprocal obligations undertaken by other Communist members of GATT are in the nature of quantity commitments (e.g., increasing imports by a certain percentage).

to introduce the maintenance of "internationally recognized" workers' rights as a qualification to the GATT system of guaranteed most-favored-nation access by member states to one another's markets.[10] This movement is animated by apparel and textiles unions which find MFN protection insufficient[11]; the possibility of a consensus on "workers' rights" for this purpose is remote, and the developing countries and many other GATT members have firmly rejected attempts to modify GATT in this direction. These facts suggest that workers' rights (and, indeed, human rights) are better promoted by other means (e.g., through other multilateral channels, such as the use of the International Labor Organization's conventions and monitoring processes, and through bilateral inducements and punishments in other areas of policy).

The temptation to make trade policy captive to sundry major and minor objectives, unmindful of costs and benefits and of alternatives, is surely to be rejected. For those who think that this temptation is only rarely indulged, I invite attention to the omnibus trade bill currently before the U.S. Congress—over 1,000 pages long, it is festooned with examples of such folly.

## The "Fairness" Issue

The insidious growth of the "fairness" issue poses a yet more disturbing threat to freer trade. The institutional changes that I proposed above should help to contain the protectionism

10. This primarily American movement has garnered some sympathetic support in Scandinavia. For historical overviews and analyses, see Charnovitz 1987 and Hansson 1983.

11. Hansson (1983) views such "social clauses" in trade regimes as instruments designed essentially to protect labor-intensive industries, and wages therein, in the developed countries. Whether such protection is indeed the outcome, and whether alternative trade policies will not procure an identical outcome at lower cost, are two of the issues he addresses.

that this issue generates on the import side. However, it is necessary also to focus on, and to counter, the protectionism that concerns about "fairness" generate on the export side. In chapter 4 I discussed how the presumption of the unfairness of foreign rivals had resulted in aggressive, bilateral efforts aimed allegedly at opening foreign markets. These efforts are often well intentioned. However, the fair-traders who engage in them are unwittingly embracing protectionism. It is hard for them to see this. They act as if they had promoted motherhood and were accused of encouraging incest. It is important, therefore, to reiterate three essential objections to bilateral approaches aimed at specific industries in specific countries[12] and to provisions targeting countries more generally.[13]

• In the bilateral confrontations already undertaken by the United States, it is essentially the United States that decides if the foreign markets are unfairly closed. Where the weak are confronted, they will concede but will be resentful. Where the strong are confronted, retaliation and trade skirmishes are a distinct possibility. The Europeans, who are strong, have indeed threatened trade wars over punitive U.S. tariffs; they have also started compiling and disseminating information about America's own unfair trading practices. All this serves the protectionist interests by creating a sense of an unfairly trading world economy in which a country that keeps its markets open appears to be denying itself indulgence while all others are given to gratification.

• The bilateral confrontations also have the demerit, stressed in chapter 4, of becoming a form of export protectionism. Faced with demands they cannot refuse, the weaker trading

12. Such an approach underlies Section 301 of the U.S. Trade Act.

13. "Super-301" provisions of this sort are found in both the Senate and the House version of the pending trade bill.

partners are likely to satisfy bilateral U.S. demands by simply taking trade away from others and giving it to the United States. This is *not* an opening of markets. It is, rather, a way of increasing U.S. exports by diverting them from more efficient suppliers who have less political clout. In chapter 4 I gave several examples of this perverse outcome in cases where the United States had undertaken bilateral, eyeball-to-eyeball trade diplomacy. The impeccable "trade-expanding" intentions of Representative Richard Gephardt, Senator John Danforth, and others would yield, not efficiently expanding global trade, but a world economy in which the politically powerful nations would expand their exports to weaker nations at the expense of less powerful but more efficient rivals. The overwhelmingly likely outcome then would be a proliferation of voluntary import expansions—discriminatory, quantitative commitments by specific countries to increase specific imports from the United States. Such expansions would recreate exports in the image of imports already plagued by the spread of discriminatory voluntary export restrictions. This would be a giant step backward.

• In addition to the protectionist fallout from the bilateral aspects of Section 301 and of "super-301" provisions that I have outlined here, the sectoral aspects of 301-type trade practices are bothersome in yet other ways. In particular, many critics have noticed that—in contrast to the GATT approach of first-difference reciprocity of concessions and advantages, which seeks such reciprocity in terms of the broad balance of concessions overall—the seeking of reciprocity by and within each sector could create demands that would be hard to accept politically and hence lead to the risk of confrontation degenerating into punitive tariffs (which would invite retaliatory tariffs). Of course, much would depend on the diplomatic skills with which such games would be played by governments caught in 301-type situations. But it cannot be denied that these skills would be sorely tried, and the perils of playing such games lie not merely in the possibility of generating trade warfare but also in the atmosphere of mutual hostility and suspicion of unfair trade (and unfair manipulation of flimsy charges of unfair trade) that such game-playing must inevitably produce.

I remain, therefore, profoundly opposed to this turn to the bilateral "open foreign markets aggressively" policies, based on exaggerated "I am more open than thou" presumptions, that afflicts current U.S. policymakers. It would be wise to pull back from these policies at the first opportunity, and to display statesmanship and commitment to the goals of a liberal trading regime.

---

*Interventions Abroad: Market Failure and Social Objectives*

Another aspect of the concern with unfair trade is the increasing tendency to object to virtually any state intervention abroad as producing a departure from fair trade among competing producers. This approach—manifest in the attitudes and positions adopted in the discussions that led up to the Tokyo Code on Subsidies, and in the national operation of countervailing-duty procedures[14]—is surely a wrongheaded one.

Any sensible economist will point out the need to distinguish between those state interventions that correct for market failure and those that create it. The former are surely desirable; they make the Darwinian struggle for markets economically more efficient and socially more productive, and they ought to be applauded rather than opposed and countervailed. Therefore, international codes and national rulings

14. Finger and Nogues (1987) and Nam (1987) offer complementary analyses of the U.S. practices with regard to this issue.

---

that reflect the belief that all export subsidies (for example) are necessarily reprehensible and destroy fair competition are based on egregious fallacies.

I would also like to see a far greater tolerance of other countries' social objectives, some of which lead to interventions in trade that the U.S. export lobbies oppose on the grounds that they are unfair. It is not surprising, for example, that Canada, Australia, and many other countries take measures to support their own arts and letters. Even the United States would be unwilling to leave cultural matters wholly to the marketplace; witness the restrictions on foreign ownership of U.S. media. And yet, in the recent negotiations on the U.S.-Canada free-trade area, the U.S. media industry's strenuous and thoughtless objections to Canada's interventions in support of Canadian cultural identity were a major source of friction.

## High Technology and "Level Playing Fields"

The fairness issue appears in a different and more persuasive guise when we consider the question of intra-sectoral "level playing fields" in the context of the few technology-intensive industries in which there are significant scale economies relative to the size of the world market. As was discussed above, export subsidization and import protection can be instruments, in such cases, for predatory expansion by a foreign rival at the expense of the domestic industry.[15]

In such cases, the objection to artificial disadvantages to one's industry resulting from disproportionate state support of the industry in other countries gains greater cogency.

---

15. This does not necessarily translate, as some eager proponents of these arguments imply, into a corresponding societal gain for the foreign country and loss for the home country.

---

Whereas a broad correspondence between national and cosmopolitan advantage may be asserted in cases of foreign state interventions aimed at correcting for market failure (e.g., the promotion of an infant industry), such an assertion generally cannot be made in the case of foreign state intervention that is predatory.[16]

Besides, as I have noted, high-technology industries are often regarded as essential to a country's economic well-being in some vague but deeply felt fashion. Hence, any significant foreign state intervention to assist them proves inflammatory.

The constellation of these economic arguments—one invoking substantial scale economies and the other significant external economies—seems to suggest that an international consensus on the desirability of achieving a *broad* intrasectoral balance of artificial advantages in a *narrow* range of such industries would be a useful supplement to the world trade regime. The emphasis, however, should not be on bilateral negotiations (in which the strong countries would browbeat the weak); it should be on multilateral procedures for determining fairly the broad balance of artificial supports in different countries in the industry in question. For example, the argument that the amount and the technological intensity of U.S. defense spending create a major advantage for American high-technology firms, which must be set against Japan's support for Japanese firms, is unlikely to be settled impartially in bilateral confrontations between the

16. Strictly speaking, cosmopolitan advantage may be consistent in specific cases with such predatory action. The reason is that, in an oligopolistic situation, *laissez faire* is a suboptimal situation. This is in contrast to the traditional competitive model, in which an optimal tariff by a country to exploit its monopoly power in trade in a predatory fashion must necessarily reduce world welfare by getting the world off the contract curve.

United States and Japan.[17] Though Japan would probably prefer to settle these disputes bilaterally, there is little doubt that multilateral negotiations and dispute-settlement procedures would be preferred by most other nations. It would certainly inhibit the hasty and often selectively self-serving finger-pointing to which some governments are prone.

## A Reminder

The new long-run pro-trade forces that I have identified, and the institutional reforms to harness them and to inhibit the protectionist forces that I have proposed, will work only haltingly if economists and policymakers do not learn how to manage international macroeconomic policies. Good microeconomics presupposes good macroeconomics. It was not for nothing that Nobel laureate James Meade's classic work on the theory of international economic policy had two volumes, one on balance-of-payments management and a second (in the proper sequence) on the theory of commercial policy. The experiences of the interwar period and the 1970s underline the importance of proper macroeconomic management if we are to be able politically to manage trade policies so as to reap the gains from trade.

But this merely underlines how the current situation offers both opportunities and vulnerabilities, calling for a skillful, long-sighted, and continuous exercise of leadership, informed by economic science and by political skills.

17. Similar arguments arise with respect to a number of other areas. For example, government funding of university-level education in the natural sciences can affect the comparative advantage in high-tech industries that need scientifically trained employees. All this emphasizes the need for policymakers to be relaxed about raising questions relating to "level playing fields."

Let me conclude by reasserting my guarded optimism in regard to the long-run prospects for keeping protectionism at bay. My mind turns back to Ragnar Nurkse, whose pessimism about the prospects for world trade was invalidated by the glorious 1950s and 1960s.[18] I hope that my optimism encounters a more indulgent future.

18. Nurkse's pessimism was expressed in his Wicksell Lectures—delivered, as it happens, at the Stockholm School of Economics, where my Ohlin Lectures were given three decades later.

# Bibliography

Arrow, Kenneth J. 1962. "The Economic Implications of Learning by Doing." *Review of Economic Studies* 29: 155–173.

Axelrod, Robert. 1981. "The Emergence of Cooperation among Egoists." *American Political Science Review* 75: 308–318.

Balassa, Bela. 1971. *The Structure of Protection in Developing Countries.* Baltimore: Johns Hopkins University Press.

Balassa, Bela, ed. 1975. *European Economic Integration.* Amsterdam: North-Holland.

Balassa, Bela. 1986. The Importance of Trade for Developing Countries. Paper presented at the World Bank–Thai Development Research Institute Conference on The Role and Interests of Developing Countries in MTN.

Balassa, Bela. 1986. "Japan's Trade Policies." *Weltwirtschaftliches Archiv* 122: 745–790.

Baldwin, David. 1986. *Economic Statecraft.* Princeton University Press.

Baldwin, Robert. 1982. The Inefficacy of Trade Policy. Princeton University Essays in International Finance, no. 150.

Baldwin, Robert. 1985a. "Inefficacy of Protection in Promoting Social Goals." *World Economy* 8: 109–118.

Baldwin, Robert. 1985b. *The Political Economy of U.S. Import Policy.* Cambridge, Mass.: MIT Press.

Bardhan, Pranab K. 1970. *Economic Growth, Development, and Foreign Trade: A Study in Pure Theory.* New York: Wiley-Interscience.

Basevi, Giorgio. 1970. "Domestic Demand and the Ability to Export." *Journal of Political Economy* 78: 330–340.

Bhagwati, Jagdish. 1968. The Theory and Practice of Commercial Policy. Princeton University Essays in International Finance, no. 8.

Bhagwati, Jagdish. 1971. "The Generalized Theory of Distortions and Welfare." In J. Bhagwati et al., eds., *Trade, Balance of Payments and Growth*. Amsterdam: North-Holland.

Bhagwati, Jagdish. 1978. *Anatomy and Consequence of Exchange Control Regimes*. Cambridge, Mass.: Ballinger.

Bhagwati, Jagdish. 1980. "Lobbying and Welfare." *Journal of Public Economics* 14: 355–363.

Bhagwati, Jagdish. 1982a. "Shifting Comparative Advantage, Protectionist Demands, and Policy Response." In J. Bhagwati, ed., *Import Competition and Response*. University of Chicago Press.

Bhagwati, Jagdish. 1982b. "Directly-Unproductive, Profit-Seeking (DUP) Activities." *Journal of Political Economy* 90: 988–1002.

Bhagwati, Jagdish, ed. 1982c. *Import Competition and Response*. University of Chicago Press.

Bhagwati, Jagdish. 1983. "DUP Activities and Rent Seeking." *Kyklos* 36: 634–637.

Bhagwati, Jagdish. 1985a. "Protectionism: Old Wine in New Bottles." *Journal of Policy Modeling* 7: 23–33.

Bhagwati, Jagdish. 1985b. "Export Promotion as a Development Strategy." In Toshio Shishido and Ryuzo Sato, eds., *Essays in Honor of Saburo Okita*. Boston: Auburn House.

Bhagwati, Jagdish. 1986a. Investing Abroad. Esmee Fairbairn Lecture, University of Lancaster.

Bhagwati, Jagdish. 1986b. Japan's Trade Problem: A Giant among Lilliputians. Japan-U.S. Center, New York University.

Bhagwati, Jagdish. 1986c. Export-Promoting Trade Strategy: Issues and Evidence. Mimeo, World Bank (VPERS). Revised version: *World Bank Research Observer* 3 (1988): 27–57.

Bhagwati, Jagdish. 1986d. "Export-Promoting Protection: Endogenous Monopoly and Price Disparity." *Pakistan Development Review*, forthcoming.

Bhagwati, Jagdish. 1986e. A Giant among Lilliputians: Japan's Long-Run Trade Problem. Japan-U.S. Business and Economic Studies, New York University.

Bhagwati, Jagdish. 1987. "VERs, Quid Pro Quo DFI and VIEs: Political-Economy-Theoretic Analyses." *International Economic Journal* 1: 1–12.

Bhagwati, Jagdish, and Elias Dinopoulos. 1986. *Quid Pro Quo* Investment and Market Structure. Paper presented to Western Economic Association Conference.

Bhagwati, Jagdish, and Douglas Irwin. 1987. "The Return of the Reciprocitarians: U.S. Trade Policy Today." *World Economy* 10: 109–130.

Bhagwati, Jagdish, and V. K. Ramaswami. 1963. "Domestic Distortions, Tariffs, and the Theory of Optimum Subsidy." *Journal of Political Economy* 71: 44–50.

Bhagwati, Jagdish, and T. N. Srinivasan. 1980. "Revenue Seeking: A Generalization of the Theory of Tariffs." *Journal of Political Economy* 88: 1069–1087.

Bhagwati, Jagdish, and T. N. Srinivasan. 1983. *Lectures on International Trade*. Cambridge, Mass.: MIT Press.

Bhagwati, Jagdish, Anne Krueger, and Richard Snape. 1987. "Introduction." *World Bank Economic Review* 1: 539–548.

Bhagwati, Jagdish, Richard Brecher, Elias Dinopoulos, and T. N. Srinivasan. 1987. "*Quid Pro Quo* Investment and Policy Intervention: A Political-Economy-Theoretic Analysis." *Journal of Development Economics* 27: 127–138.

Blomström, Magnus. 1986. *Swedish Multinationals Abroad*. New York: NBER.

Borner, Silvio. 1986. *Internationalization of Industry*. Berlin: Springer-Verlag.

Borner, Silvio, and F. Wehrle. 1984. *Die Sechste Schweitz*. Zurich: Orell Fussli.

Bovard, James. 1987. "U.S. Fair Trade Laws Are Anything But." *Wall Street Journal*, June 3.

Bradford, Sarah. 1984. *Disraeli*. New York: Stein and Day.

Brander, James. 1986. "Rationales for Strategic Trade and Industrial Policy." In Krugman 1986.

Brander, James, and Barbara Spencer. 1981. "Tariffs and the Extraction of Foreign Monopoly Rents under Potential Entry." *Canadian Journal of Economics* 14: 371–389. Reprinted in Bhagwati 1987c.

Brecher, Richard, and Jagdish Bhagwati. 1987. "Voluntary Export Restrictions versus Import Restrictions: A Welfare-Theoretic Comparison." In H. Kierzkowski, ed., *Essays in Honor of W. M. Corden.* Oxford: Blackwell.

Buchanan, James. 1980. "Rent Seeking and Profit Seeking." In J. Buchanan et al., eds., *Towards a General Theory of the Rent Seeking Society.* College Station: Texas A&M Press.

Carr, Edward H. 1951. *The New Society.* Boston: Beacon.

Cassing, James, Timothy McKeown, and Jack Ochs. 1986. "The Political Economy of the Tariff Cycle." *American Political Science Review* 80: 843–862.

Chaikin, Sol. 1982. "Trade, Investment, and Deindustrialization: Myth and Reality." *Foreign Affairs* 60: 836–851.

Charnovitz, Steve. 1987. "International Trade and Worker Rights." *SAIS Review* 7: 185–198.

Cheh, John. 1974. "United States Concessions in the Kennedy Round and Short-Run Labor Adjustment Costs." *Journal of International Economics* 4: 323–340.

Cho, Yoon Je. 1987. Developing Country Strategy for International Trade in Financial Services—Lessons from the Opening of the Korean Insurance Market. Mimeo, World Bank. *World Bank Economic Review,* forthcoming.

Cohen, Stephen, and John Zysman. 1987. *Manufacturing Matters: The Myth of the Post-Industrial Economy.* New York: Basic Books.

Colander, David C., ed. 1984. *Neoclassical Political Economy.* Cambridge, Mass.: Ballinger.

Corden, W. M. 1971. "The Effects of Trade on the Rate of Growth." In J. Bhagwati et al., eds., *Trade, Balance of Payments, and Growth.* Amsterdam: North-Holland.

Corden, W. M. 1974. *Trade Policy and Economic Welfare.* Oxford University Press.

Crouzet, Francois. 1982. *The Victorian Economy.* London: Methuen.

Destler, I. M. 1986. *American Trade Politics: System Under Stress.* Washington, D.C.: Institute for International Economics.

Dickey, William L. 1979. "The Pricing of Imports into the United States." *Journal of World Trade Law* 13: 238–256.

Dinopoulos, Elias. 1987. "*Quid Pro Quo* Foreign Investment and Market Structure." Paper presented at World Bank Conference on Political Economy: Theory and Policy.

Dinopoulos, Elias, and M. Kreinin. 1986. Import Quotas and VERs: A Comparative Analysis in a Three-Country Framework. Mimeo, Michigan State University.

Dirksen, Erik. 1987. "What If the Soviet Union Applies to Join the GATT?" *World Economy* 10: 228–230.

Dixit, Avinash. 1983. "International Trade Policy for Oligopolistic Industries." *Economic Journal*, supplement, 94: 1–16. Reprinted in Bhagwati 1987c.

Eaton, Jonathan, and Gene Grossman. 1986. "Optimal Trade and Industrial Policy under Oligopoly." *Quarterly Journal of Economics* 101: 383–406. Reprinted in Bhagwati 1987c.

Eichengreen, Barry. 1986. The Political Economy of the Smoot-Hawley Tariff. NBER Working Paper no. 2001.

Feenstra, Robert. 1986. "Trade Policy with Several Goods and Market Linkages." *Journal of International Economics* 20: 249–267.

Feenstra, Robert, and Jagdish Bhagwati. 1982. "Tariff Seeking and the Efficient Tariff." In J. Bhagwati, ed., *Import Competition and Response*. University of Chicago Press.

Findlay, Ronald. 1984. "Protection and Growth in a Dual Economy." In Mark Gersowitz et al., eds., *The Theory and Experience of Economic Development*. London: Allen and Unwin.

Finger, J. M. 1979. "Trade Liberalization: A Public Choice Perspective." In R. C. Amacher, G. Haberler, and T. D. Willett, eds., *Challenges to a Liberal International Economic Order*. Washington, D.C.: American Enterprise Institute.

Finger, J. M. 1982. "Incorporating the Gains from Trade into Policy." *World Economy* 5: 367–377.

Finger, J. M., and J. Nogues. 1987. "International Control of Subsidies and Countervailing Duties." *World Bank Economic Review* 1: 707–726.

Finger, J. M., H. Keith Hall, and Douglas R. Nelson. 1982. "The Political Economy of Administered Protection." *American Economic Review* 72: 452–466.

Folsom, Michael, and Steven Lubar, eds. 1980. *The Philosophy of Manufactures: Early Debates Over Industrialization in the United States*. Cambridge, Mass.: MIT Press.

Friedman, Milton, and Anna Schwartz. 1963. *A Monetary History of the United States, 1867–1960*. Princeton University Press.

Gash, Norman. 1972. *Sir Robert Peel*. London: Longman.

Goldstein, Judith. 1986. "The Political Economy of Trade: Institutions of Protection." *American Political Science Review* 80: 161–184.

Goldstein, Judith, and Stephen Krasner. 1984. "Unfair Trade Practices: The Case for a Differential Response." *American Economic Review* 74: 282–287.

Graaff, J. de V. 1949–50. "On Optimum Tariff Structures. *Review of Economic Studies* 17: 47–59.

Grossman, Gene M. 1986. "Strategic Export Promotion: A Critique." In Krugman 1986.

Hall, H. Keith, and Douglas Nelson. 1987. Institutional Structure in the Political Economy of Protection: Legislative vs. Administrative Protection. Mimeo.

Hansson, Göte. 1983. *Social Clauses and International Trade*. New York: St. Martin's.

Helleiner, G. K. 1977. "Transnational Enterprises and the New Political Economy of United States Trade Policy." *Oxford Economic Papers* 29: 102–116.

Hindley, Brian. 1987. "GATT Safeguards and Voluntary Export Restraints: What Are the Interests of Developing Countries?" *World Bank Economic Review* 1: 689–706.

Hirschman, Albert. 1958. *The Strategy of Economic Development*. New Haven: Yale University Press.

Hobson, J. A. 1919. *Richard Cobden—The International Man*. New York: Holt.

Holzman, Franklyn. 1983. "Dumping in the Centrally Planned Economies: The Polish Golf Cart Case 133." In Padma Desai, ed., *Marxism, Central Planning, and the Soviet Economy*. Cambridge, Mass.: MIT Press.

Hufbauer, Gary, and Howard Rosen. 1986. *Trade Policy for Troubled Industries*. Washington, D.C.: Institute for International Economics.

Hufbauer, G., and J. Schott. 1985. *Trading for Growth*. Washington, D.C.: Institute for International Economics.

Hughes, Gordon, and David Newberry. 1986. "Protection and Developing Countries' Exports of Manufactures." *Economic Policy* 2: 409–440.

Hughes, Helen, and Anne Krueger. 1984. "Effects of Protection in Developed Countries on Developing Countries." In Robert Baldwin and Anne Krueger, eds., *The Structure and Evolution of Recent U.S. Trade Policy*. University of Chicago Press.

International Monetary Fund. 1982. *Supplement on Trade Statistics*. Washington, D.C.

International Monetary Fund. 1985. *International Financial Statistics*. Washington, D.C.

International Monetary Fund. 1987. *International Financial Statistics*. Washington, D.C.

Irwin, Douglas. 1987. Welfare Effects of British Free Trade: Debate and Evidence from the 1840s. Presented to Mid-West International Economics Meetings. Ann Arbor.

Isaacs, Asher. 1948. *International Trade Tariff and Commercial Policies*. Chicago: Irwin.

Jackson, John. 1969. *World Trade and the Law of GATT*. Charlottesville: Michie.

Johnson, Harry. 1953. "Optimum Tariffs and Retaliation." *Review of Economic Studies* 21: 142–153.

Johnson, Harry. 1955. "Economic Expansion and International Trade." *Manchester School of Economics and Social Science* 23: 95–112.

Johnson, Harry. 1965. "Optimal Trade Intervention in the Presence of Domestic Distortions." In R. Caves et al., eds., *Trade, Growth, and the Balance of Payments*. New York: Rand McNally.

Jones, Ronald. 1967. "International Capital Movements and the Theory of Tariffs and Trade." *Quarterly Journal of Economics* 81: 1–38.

Kaldor, Nicholas. 1966. *The Causes of the Slow Economic Growth of the United Kingdom*. Cambridge University Press.

Kemp, Murray C. 1966. "The Gain from International Trade and Investment: A Neo-Heckscher-Ohlin Approach." *American Economic Review* 61: 788–809.

Kennedy, Kevin C. 1987. "The Accession of the Soviet Union to GATT." *Journal of World Trade Law* 21: 23–39.

Keohane, Robert O., 1980. "The Theory of Hegemonic Stability and Changes in International Economic Regimes, 1967–1977." In Ole Holsti, Randolph M. Siverson, and Alexander L. George, eds., *Changes in the International System*. Boulder: Westwood.

Keynes, J. M., ed. 1926. *Official Papers of Alfred Marshall*. London: Macmillan.

Keynes, J. M. 1936. *The General Theory of Interest, Employment and Money*. London: Macmillan.

Keynes, J. M. 1974. "The International Control of Raw Materials." *Journal of International Economics* 4: 299–316.

Kindleberger, Charles P. 1981. "Dominance and Leadership in the International Economy: Exploitation, Public Goods and Free Riders." *International Studies Quarterly* 25: 242–254.

Kindleberger, Charles P. 1982–83. "Cycles in Protection and Free Trade." *Le Temps Strategique* 3: 95–100.

Kindleberger, Charles P. 1986. *The World in Depression: 1929–1939*. Revised edition. Berkeley: University of California Press.

Krasner, Stephen. 1976. "State Power and the Structure of International Trade." *World Politics* 28: 317–347.

Krueger, Anne. 1974, "The Political Economy of the Rent-Seeking Society." *American Economic Review* 64: 291–303.

Krueger, Anne. 1978. *Foreign Trade Regimes and Economic Development: Liberalization Attempts and Consequences*. Cambridge, Mass.: Ballinger.

Krugman, Paul R. 1984. "Import Protection as Export Promotion." In H. Kierzkowski, ed., *Monopolistic Competition and International Trade*. Oxford University Press.

Krugman, Paul R., ed. 1986. *Strategic Trade Policy and the New International Economics*. Cambridge, Mass.: MIT Press.

Laird, Sam, and J. Michael Finger. 1986. Protection in Developed and Developing Countries: An Overview. Mimeo, World Bank, Washington, D.C.

Lavergne, Real. 1983. *The Political Economy of U.S. Tariffs: An Empirical Investigation*. New York: Academic.

Lawrence, Robert Z. 1987. "Imports in Japan: Closed Minds or Markets?" *Brookings Papers on Economic Activity* 2: 517–554.

Lawrence, Robert Z., and Robert Litan. 1986. *Saving Free Trade: A Pragmatic Approach*. Washington, D.C.: Brookings Institution.

Liepmann, H. 1938. *Tariff Levels and the Economic Unity of Europe*. New York: Macmillan.

Linder, Staffan Burenstam. 1961. *An Essay on Trade and Transformation*. New York: Wiley.

Linder, Staffan Burenstam. 1986. *The Pacific Century*. Stanford University Press.

Lipsey, Robert E., and Irving B. Kravis. 1986. The Competitiveness and Comparative Advantage of U.S. Multinationals, 1957–1983. NBER Working Paper no. 2051.

Little, Ian, Tibor Scitovsky, and Maurice Scott. 1970. *Industry and Trade in Some Developing Countries*. London: Oxford University Press.

McArthur, John, and Stephen Marks. 1988. "Constituent Interest vs. Legislator Ideology: The Role of Opportunity Cost." *Economic Inquiry*, forthcoming.

McCloskey, Donald N. 1980. "Magnanimous Albion: Free Trade and British National Income, 1841–1881." *Explorations in Economic History* 17: 303–320.

MacIntyre, Alasdair. 1985. *A Short History of Ethics*. New York: Macmillan.

McMillan, John. 1986. *Game Theory in International Economics*. New York: Harwood.

Magee, Stephen. 1980. "Three Simple Tests of the Stolper-Samuelson Theorem." In P. Oppenheimer, ed., *Issues in International Economics*. London: Oriel.

Mann, Catherine. 1987. "Protection and Retaliation: Changing the Rules of the Game." *Brookings Papers on Economic Activity* 1: 311–348.

Mayer, Wolfgang. 1984. "The Infant-Export Industry Argument." *Canadian Journal of Economics* 17: 249–269.

Meade, James. 1951. *Trade and Welfare: The Theory of International Economic Policy*, vol. 2. London: Oxford University Press.

Messerlin, Patrick A. 1987. The Long Term Evolution of the EC Antidumping Law: Some Lessons for the New AD Laws in LDCs. Mimeo, World Bank.

Michaely, Michael. 1977. "Exports and Growth: An Empirical Investigation." *Journal of Development Economics* 4: 49–53.

Miller, Michael. 1985. "Big U.S. Semiconductor Makers Expected to Sue over 'Dumping' of Japanese Chips." *Wall Street Journal*, October 1.

Nam, Chong-Hyun. 1987. "Export-Promoting Subsidies, Countervailing Threats, and the General Agreement on Tariffs and Trade." *World Bank Economic Review* 1: 727–744.

Nelson, Douglas. 1987. The Domestic Political Preconditions of U.S. Trade Policy: Liberal Structure and Protectionist Dynamics. Paper presented at Conference on Political Economy of Trade: Theory and Policy, World Bank, Washington, D.C.

Noland, Marcus. 1987. An Econometric Model of the Volume of International Trade. Mimeo, Institute for International Economics.

Norall, Christopher. 1986. "New Trends in Anti-Dumping Practice in Brussels." *World Economy* 9: 97–110.

Nurkse, Ragnar. 1959. *Patterns of Trade and Development.* Stockholm: Almquist and Wicksell.

Ohlin, Bertil. 1933. *Interregional and International Trade.* Cambridge, Mass.: Harvard University Press.

Olson, Mancur. 1965. *The Logic of Collective Action: Public Goods and the Theory of Groups.* Cambridge, Mass.: Harvard University Press.

Packenham, Robert A. 1973. *Liberal America and the Third World: Political Development Ideas in Foreign Aid and Social Science.* Princeton University Press.

Pareto, Vilfredo. 1927. *Manual of Political Economy.* New York: A. M. Kelley.

Parker, Charles S., ed. 1899. *Sir Robert Peel from His Private Papers*, vol. 3. London: John Murray.

Pastor, Robert. 1983. "The Cry-and-Sigh Syndrome: Congress and Trade Policy." In A. Schick, ed., *Making Economic Policy in Congress.* Washington, D.C.: American Enterprise Institute.

Pattanaik, Prasanta. 1974. "Trade, Distribution, and Savings." *Journal of International Economics* 4: 77–82.

Pomfret, R. 1975. "Some Interrelationships between Import Substitution and Export Promotion in a Small Open Economy." *Weltwirtschaftliches Archiv* 111: 714–727.

---

Prebisch, Raul. 1952. Problemas Teoricos y Practicos del Crecimiento Economico. United Nations Economic Commission for Latin America.

Robinson, Joan. 1947. *Essays in the Theory of Employment*. Oxford: Blackwell.

Rodriguez, Carlos Alfredo. 1974. "The Non-equivalence of Tariffs and Quotas under Retaliation." *Journal of International Economics* 4: 295–298.

Rodrik, Dani. 1987. Import Competition and Trade Policy in Developing Countries. Mimeo, John F. Kennedy School of Government, Harvard University.

Rosenstein-Rodan, Paul N. R. 1943. "Problems of the Industrialization of Eastern and South-Eastern Europe." *Economic Journal* 53: 202–211.

Ruggie, John. 1982. "International Regimes, Transactions, and Change: Embedded Liberalism in the Postwar Economic Order." *International Organization* 36: 379–415.

Sathirathai, Surakiart, and Ammar Siamwalla. 1987. "GATT Law, Agricultural Trade, and Developing Countries: Lessons from Two Case Studies." *World Bank Economic Review* 1: 595–618.

Saul, S. B. 1965. "The Export Economy: 1870–1914." *Yorkshire Bulletin of Economic and Social Research* 17: 5–18.

Saxonhouse, Gary. 1983. "The Micro- and Macroeconomics of Foreign Sales to Japan." In William R. Cline, ed., *Trade Policy for the 1980s*. Cambridge, Mass.: MIT Press.

Schattschneider, E. E. 1935. *Politics, Pressures, and the Tariff*. New York: Prentice-Hall.

Scitovsky, T. 1941. "A Reconsideration of the Theory of Tariffs." *Review of Economic Studies* 9: 89–110.

Seabury, Paul. 1983. "Industrial Policy and National Defense." *Journal of Contemporary Studies* 6: 5–15.

Servan-Schreiber, Jean-Jacques. 1968. *The American Challenge*. New York: Atheneum.

Smith, Adam. 1776. *The Wealth of Nations*. Cannan edition. New York: Modern Library, 1937.

Snape, Richard H. 1987. Bilateral-Multilateral Tension in Trade Policy. Paper presented at Western Economic Association Meetings, Vancouver.

Solow, Robert. 1956. "A Contribution to the Theory of Economic Growth." *Quarterly Journal of Economics* 70: 65–94.

Spencer, Barbara J. 1986. "What Should Trade Policy Target?" In Krugman 1986.

Swedenborg, Birgitta. 1982. *Svensk industri utlandet: En analys ar drivkrafter och effekter.* Stockholm: Industrieris Utrednignsinstitut.

Tackacs, Wendy. 1981. "Pressures for Protectionism: An Empirical Analysis." *Economic Inquiry* 19: 687–693.

Tarr, David, and Morris Morkre. 1984. *Aggregate Costs to the United States of Tariffs and Quotas on Imports: General Tariff Cuts and Removal of Quotas on Automobiles, Steel, Sugar, and Textiles.* Washington, D.C.: Bureau of Economics, Federal Trade Commission.

Temin, Peter. 1976. *Did Monetary Forces Cause the Great Depression?* New York: Norton.

Tullock, Gordon C. 1967. "The Welfare Costs of Tariffs, Monopolies, and Theft." *Western Economic Journal* 5: 224–232.

Tumlir, Jan. 1985. *Protectionism: Trade Policy in Democratic Societies.* Washington, D.C.: American Enterprise Institute.

UNCTAD. 1983. *Handbook of International Trade and Development Statistics.* Geneva.

UNCTAD. 1984. *Handbook of International Trade and Development Statistics.* Geneva.

UNCTAD. 1987. *Handbook of International Trade and Development Statistics.* Geneva.

White, Theodore. 1985. "The Danger from Japan." *New York Times Magazine,* July 28.

Willett, Thomas. 1984. "International Trade and Protectionism." *Contemporary Policy Issues* 4: 1–5.

Wolff, Alan. 1983. "Need for New GATT Rules to Govern Safeguard Actions." In William Cline, ed., *Trade Policy for the 1980s.* Cambridge, Mass.: MIT Press.

Wong, Kar-yiu. 1987. Optimal Threat of Trade Restriction and *Quid Pro Quo* Foreign Investment. Presented at World Bank Conference on Political Economy: Theory and Policy.

World Bank. 1987. *World Development Report.* New York: Oxford University Press.

# Name Index

Axelrod, R., 109

Balassa, B., 7, 70
Baldwin, D., 122
Baldwin, R., 56
Balogh, T., 97
Bovard, J., 52
Bowley, A., 31

Callahan, J., 110
Cannan, E., 31
Carlyle, T., 17
Carr, E., 92
Chaikin, S., 64
Cho, Y., 84
Cobden, R., 18, 29
Cohen, S., 113

Destler, I., 85
Dickey, W., 51
Disraeli, B., 18

Edgeworth, F., 24, 31

Finger, J., 53
Friedman, M., 35, 97, 98

Galbraith, J., 22
Gladstone, W., 30
Grossman, G., 107

Haberler, G., xi
Harrod, R., xi
Heckscher, E., xi
Helleiner, G., 77

Johnson, H., xi

Kaldor, N., 110–111
Kennan, G., 39
Keynes, J., 2, 17
Kindleberger, C., 40
Kravis, I., 75
Krueger, A., 103

Lavergne, R., 77
Lawrence, R., 70
Linder, S., 5, 65
Lippmann, W., 65
Lipsey, R., 75

Marshall, A., 26, 30–31
Meade, J., 129
Messerlin, P., 50

Mill, J., 18, 24, 25, 112
Mondale, W., 64

Nelson, D., 39
Nogues, J., 53
Noland, M., 69
Norall, C., 50
Nurkse, R., 89, 101, 130

Ohlin, B., xi–xii
Ohlin, G., xii

Pareto, V., 72
Peel, R., 18, 20, 27
Prebisch, R., 52

Ricardo, D., 24
Rosenstein-Rodan, P., 89

Saxonhouse, G., 69
Servan-Schreiber, J., 74
Srinivasan, T., 104
Smith, A., 24, 26
Smith, F., 51

Tinbergen, J., 122
Tumlir, J., 59, 120

White, T., 64
Wicksell, K., xi
Wilde, O., 91

Zysman, J., 113

# Subject Index

Adjustment assistance, 118ff
Administered Protection, 43, 53.
  *See also* Countervailing duties;
  Anti-dumping duties
Agriculture, 9–10, 13, 81, 91ff,
  114
Anti-dumping duties (ADs), 35,
  44–45, 48–53, 82, 115–116

Bretton Woods, 1
Britain, 2, 18, 20, 27, 29–30, 34,
  37, 54, 63–68, 110–111

Canada, 12, 48, 54, 86
Chrysler, 117
Congress, U.S., 23, 41–42, 70,
  78, 82, 85, 123
Corn Laws, 18, 29
Countervailing duties (CVDs),
  35, 44–45, 48–53, 82, 115–116,
  126

Deindustrialization, 62, 64–65,
  110
Direct foreign investment (DFI),
  71, 73–77, 79–80
Directly unproductive profit-
  seeking (DUP), 100, 102ff

Domestic distortions. *See* Market
  failure
Dumping, 34–35

Effective exchange rate (EER),
  94ff
Executive, U.S., 23, 38–39, 41–
  43, 58, 68, 80
Export pessimism, 89ff
Export subsidies, 34–35, 95–96,
  106ff, 127
Externalities. *See* Market failure;
  Infant industries
European Economic Community
  (EEC), 3, 7, 11, 45, 48, 50

Free trade, 18, 22–27, 29, 31–35,
  38–39, 57, 59, 67, 72, 94–95,
  104

General Agreement on Tariffs
  and Trade (GATT), 1, 3, 9,
  11–12, 23, 33, 35, 40–41, 43,
  47, 51, 58, 80–81, 91, 120–123,
  125
Germany, 27, 66–67
Great Depression, 20–22
Government, 94ff

Ideas, 102ff
Ideology, 17–18, 20, 22–23, 38–39, 41–42, 54, 87ff
Imperfect competition, 105ff
Import substitution, 12, 73, 88ff
India, 93, 100
Industrialization. *See* Manufacturing
Infant industries, 25, 30, 32, 91, 96–97, 128
Institutions, 17–18, 23, 41–42, 54, 115ff
Interests, 17–18, 37, 41–42, 54, 75ff, 80–81, 86
International Monetary Fund (IMF), 1, 90
Intra-industry trade, 56–57
Israel, 12, 85

Japan, 50, 53–54, 62–69, 78–80, 82–85, 97–98, 100, 108–109, 128–129

Learning by doing, 96–97

Macroeconomics, 1, 61, 70–71, 85, 129
Manufacturing, 10, 13, 63–64, 91ff, 110–114
Market failure, 25, 32, 33–34, 91–92, 95–97, 102, 104ff, 111, 126–128
Mercantilism, 24
Ministry of International Trade and Industry (MITI), 100–101
Most Favored Nation (MFN), 11–12, 47, 80–81, 121, 123
Multifibre Agreement (MFA). *See* Textiles
Multinationals. *See* Direct foreign investment

Newly exporting countries (NECs), 63
Newly industrializing countries (NICs), 41, 62–64
Nontariff barriers (NTBs), 3, 10–11, 13, 43–45, 47, 53–54, 56

Organization of Petroleum Exporting Countries (OPEC), 23, 54, 70

Poland, 51
Prescriptive and proscriptive governments, 98–101
Primary production. *See* Agriculture

Reciprocity, 30–31, 35–36, 68, 125
Rent seeking. *See* Directly unproductive profit-seeking
Retaliation, 25–26, 30–33, 108–110, 124

Safeguards, 61, 116, 118–119
Services, 64, 81, 111–114
Smoot-Hawley tariff, 22–23, 32, 41–42, 87
South Korea, 54, 62, 84, 93
Soviet Union. *See* Union of Soviet Socialist Republics

Taiwan, 62, 94
Textiles, 11–12, 44, 78
Trade and growth, 4–5, 7–9, 54–55, 63
Trade liberalization (postwar), 31, 37, 39–40, 41–43, 47, 81, 87, 93
and developed countries, 1, 3–4, 6–12, 20, 22, 40
and developing countries, 12–13, 40, 88ff

Unfair trade (Section 301), 34ff,
    82, 84, 123–126
Union of Soviet Socialist Repub-
    lics (USSR), 37, 121–122
United Kingdom. *See* Britain
United Nations Conference on
    Trade and Development
    (UNCTAD), 13, 44
United States, 2–3, 9–12, 22, 27,
    31, 34, 36–40, 48, 51–54, 62–
    68, 70–71, 78–86, 108–109,
    121, 124–125, 128–129

Voluntary export restraints
    (VERs), 11, 44–45, 53, 57–59,
    63, 82–83, 117, 119–120
Voluntary import expansions
    (VIEs), 82–84, 109

World Bank, 1